# How to Become a Christian

by John Isaac Edwards and Larry R. Ping II

© 2018 One Stone Press.
All rights reserved. No part of this book may be reproduced in any form without written permission of the publisher.

Published by:
One Stone Press
979 Lovers Lane
Bowling Green, KY 42103

Printed in the United States of America

ISBN: 978-1-941422-34-2

www.onestone.com

# Table of Contents

**Lesson 1:** What Is a Christian? ................................................................... 5

**Lesson 2:** Why Become a Christian? ........................................................ 13

**Lesson 3:** Understanding Sin ................................................................... 21

**Lesson 4:** Hearing the Word of God ........................................................ 31

**Lesson 5:** The Need for Belief .................................................................. 41

**Lesson 6:** The Importance of Repentance .............................................. 49

**Lesson 7:** The Call for Confession ............................................................ 57

**Lesson 8:** The Necessity of Baptism ........................................................ 65

**Lesson 9:** The Action of Baptism ............................................................. 71

**Lesson 10:** Why Do Some Wait? ............................................................... 77

**Lesson 11:** Now That You're a Christian .................................................. 85

**Lesson 12:** Responsibilities of a Christian .............................................. 93

**Lesson 13:** Helping Others Become Christians .................................... 101

## Lesson 1

# What Is a Christian?

Welcome to this series of lessons designed to teach one how to become a Christian. The most important thing in life is to become a Christian and be faithful until death. In this first lesson we are asking the question, "What is a Christian?"

### In your own words

Before going any further in this lesson, think about what a Christian is. Now, in the box below, write what you think a Christian is.

### Memory Verse

....And the disciples were first called **Christians** in Antioch.

- Acts 11:26

### Use of the word "Christian"

The Bible uses the word "Christian" three times. All three of these are in the New Testament.

1. **Acts 11:26:** the _____ were first called _____ in Antioch.

2. **Acts 26:28:** King Agrippa said unto Paul, "...You almost persuade me to become a _____."

3. **1 Peter 4:16:** Yet if anyone suffers as a _____, let him not be ashamed, but let him glorify God in this matter.

It was prophesied in the Old Testament that the Lord's people would be called by a new name (Isaiah 56:5; 62:2; 65:15). This is fulfilled in the name "Christian."

## A Christian is not...

The word "Christian" is often abused and misused today. Many are called Christians who simply are not Christians as the Bible teaches. The following things do not make one a Christian:

1. **Just being a good person.** Some may think that if a person lives a good life (he does not use bad language, he honors and obeys his parents, he does not cheat or steal, he is kind to others), then that person is a Christian. These things are true of a Christian, but it takes more than just being a good person to make one a Christian. Cornelius was a good person. Read Acts 10:2 and list four things which show Cornelius was a good person:

   _____
   _____
   _____
   _____

   Although Cornelius was a good person, he was not yet a Christian. He was spiritually lost and had to hear words by which he would be saved (Acts 11:14).

2. **Just attending church services.** There may be some who think that because they attend church services every week that they are a Christian. Christians do assemble regularly to

> ...and he will speak **words** to you by which you **will be saved**, you and all your household.
>
> - Acts 11:14

worship God and study His word (Hebrews 10:25; John 4:24; 2 Timothy 2:15), but just being present when Christians are together does not mean that you are a Christian too.

3. **Just believing in Jesus.** A common definition of a Christian is anyone who believes in Jesus Christ. Yes, a Christian believes in Jesus. Jesus said, "...if you do not believe that I am He, you will die in your sins" (John 8:24). Remember King Agrippa? Paul said he knew that Agrippa believed (Acts 26:27), but was Agrippa a Christian? _____ Why or why not? _____

   It takes more than just believing to make one a Christian. What did James say about faith without works? (James 2:14-26)
   _____

> King Agrippa, do you **believe** the Prophets? I know that you do.
>
> - Acts 26:27

4. **Just having parents who are Christians.** Some things are inherited or passed down from our parents (such as the color of our eyes and hair, the shape of our nose, our height, our last name, and the list goes on). Just because your parents are Christians does not automatically make you a Christian. Our parents can teach us the word of God, set a good example before us and encourage us to do what is right, but becoming a Christian is a decision that we must make for ourselves. The Ethiopian treasurer said, "See, here is water. What hinders _____ from being baptized?" (Acts 8:36). Saul of Tarsus asked, "Lord, what do You want _____ to do?" (Acts 9:6). The Philippian jailor asked, "Sirs, what must _____ do to be saved?" (Acts 16:30). You can become a Christian even though your parents

may not be Christians. Jesus said, "He who loves father or mother more than Me is not worthy of Me" (Matthew 10:37).

5. **Just saying a prayer.** Many are taught that when we say a prayer like this—"Lord Jesus, I confess that I am a sinner. I receive you into my heart as my personal Lord and Saviour" (known as the "sinner's prayer")—that we are then saved and become a Christian. Both Saul and Cornelius prayed unto God (Acts 9:11; 10:2), but were they saved by praying? _____ Why or why not? _____
_____

(Acts 9:6; 10:6). Prayer is not something one does to become a Christian, but is a right and privilege one has when he becomes a Christian (Ephesians 6:18; Philippians 4:6)!

6. **Just feeling that you are a Christian.** What if someone says, "I am a Christian. I know I am a Christian; I feel it in my heart"?
_____
_____

Our feelings can deceive us. Jacob felt that his son Joseph was dead and mourned for him many days (Genesis 37:31-35), but was he really dead? _____ The wise man Solomon said, "There is a way that seems right to a man, but its end is the way of death" (Proverbs 14:12).

## A Christian is...

Now that we have learned what a Christian is not, let's take a look at what the Bible says a Christian is.

1. **A disciple of Jesus Christ.** Who were first called Christians in Antioch?
_____

> Be anxious for nothing, but in everything by **prayer** and **supplication** with **thanksgiving** let your requests be made known to God.
> - Philippians 4:6

**LESSON 1** What Is a Christian?

A disciple is a learner and follower of another. The disciples of John, for example, were those who learned and followed after John the Baptist (Matthew 9:14). Disciples of Jesus Christ are those who learn and follow after Christ. Being a disciple of Christ involves being like Christ (Matthew 10:24-25). What did Christ leave us? _____ (1 Peter 2:21) Read Luke 14:26-33, where Jesus teaches about being His disciple. Are there some who cannot be Jesus' disciple? _____ To be a disciple of Jesus, we must be willing to leave all to follow Christ.

2. **A pilgrim.** When Peter began his first letter to early Christians, he addressed it "To the _____ of the Dispersion in Pontus, Galatia, Cappadocia, Asia, and Bithynia" (1 Peter 1:1). In 1 Peter 2:11 he wrote, "Beloved, I beg you as _____ and _____, abstain from fleshly lusts which war against the soul." Read Hebrews 11:9-10, 13-16. What does it mean to be a pilgrim on the earth? _____ _____

   As Christians, this world is not our home. "For our _____ is in heaven, from which we also eagerly wait for the Saviour, the Lord Jesus Christ" (Philippians 3:20).

3. **Elect of God.** Peter further described Christians as "_____ according to the foreknowledge of God the Father" (1 Peter 1:2). To elect is to choose. Every four years, in the United States, we elect or choose a President. To be elect of God is to be chosen by God. Christians, therefore, are God's chosen, special people. 1 Peter 2:9-10 says, "But you are a

> For you have been called for this **purpose**, since Christ also suffered for you, leaving you an **example** for you to **follow** in His steps…
>
> - 1 Peter 2:21

> For all of you who were **baptized** into Christ have **clothed** yourselves with Christ.
>
> - Galatians 3:27

_____ generation, a royal priesthood, a holy nation, His own special people, that you may proclaim the _____ of Him who called you out of _____ into His marvelous _____; who once were not a people but are now the people of God, who had not obtained mercy but now have obtained mercy." Ephesians 1:3-4 teaches that we are chosen in _____, where we are blessed with every spiritual blessing in the heavenly places. Now read Galatians 3:27 to learn how one gets into Christ. _____
_____

"Baptized into" Galatians 3:27 → **Christians** — **God's chosen, special people**

4.  **Begotten again to a living hope.** Peter further described Christians saying, "Blessed be the God and Father of our Lord Jesus Christ, who according to His abundant mercy has _____ us again to a living hope through the resurrection of Jesus Christ from the dead" (1 Peter 1:3). What does it mean to be begotten again?_____
    _____

    Christians are those who have "been born again, not of corruptible seed but incorruptible, through the word of God which lives and abides forever" (1 Peter 1:23). Jesus talked to Nicodemus, a ruler of the Jews, about being born again in John 3:1-8. What do you learn from Jesus' teaching about the new birth?

_____
_____
_____

When you are born again, baptized into Jesus Christ, you have "...hope of eternal life which God, who cannot lie, promised before time began" (Titus 1:2).

5. **Redeemed with the precious blood of Christ.** Again Peter wrote of Christians, "knowing that you were not _____ with corruptible things, like silver or gold, from your aimless conduct received by tradition from your fathers, but with the precious _____ of Christ, as of a lamb without _____ and without _____" (1 Peter 1:18-19). What does it mean to be redeemed? _____
_____
Why did Christ give Himself for us? _____
_____
(Titus 2:14). A Christian, having been redeemed or purchased with the precious blood of Christ (Acts 20:28), belongs to Christ and is of great value!

6. **One who has purified his soul in obeying the truth.** 1 Peter 1:22 records, "Since you have _____ your souls in obeying the truth through the Spirit..." You have within you a soul, worth more than the whole world (Matthew 16:26). It can be saved or it can be lost! Sin, which is defined as all unrighteousness (1 John 5:17), causes the soul to become unclean or impure in the sight of God. When that happens, the soul must be purified or made wholly clean. This takes place

> For what will it profit a man if he gains the **whole world** and forfeits his **soul**? Or what will a man give in **exchange** for his soul?
> - Matthew 16:26

when you obey the truth, the word of God. Hebrews 5:9 teaches that Christ is "the author of eternal salvation to all who _____ Him." Will you obey Him?

## Some questions from our study

1. What is the most important thing in life? _____
   _____
   _____

2. What are the three places in the New Testament where the word "Christian" is used? _____
   _____

3. Being a Christian involves more than most people realize. What are examples of some who are not Christians? _____
   _____
   _____

4. How does the Bible describe a Christian? List scripture. _____
   _____
   _____
   _____

## Lesson 2

# Why Become a Christian?

In our last lesson, we learned what a Christian is. In this lesson, we are asking the question, "Why become a Christian?"

### Why some do not become Christians

Even though God loves everyone (John 3:16), Jesus died for everyone (Hebrews 2:9) and the gospel is for everyone (Mark 16:15-16), not everyone will become a Christian. In fact Jesus taught, "_____ is the gate and _____ is the way that leads to destruction, and there are _____ who go in by it" (Matthew 7:13). Let's notice why it is that some do not become Christians. Some do not become Christians because:

1. **They have not been taught.** Those who become Christians are those who hear and learn. Jesus taught, "No one can come to Me unless the Father who sent me draws him; and I will raise him up at the last day" (John 6:44). Now read John 6:45 to learn how the Father draws us. _____

    It is sad, but there are those who have never heard and learned about "the way, the truth, and the life" (John 14:6). Some have not been taught the need to become Christians and do not know about the spiritual blessings in Jesus Christ.

2. **They do not believe.** If a person does not believe, he never will become a Christian.

> **Memory Verse**
>
> For what **profit** is it to a man if he gains the whole world, and **loses** his own soul? Or what will a man give in **exchange** for his **soul**?
>
> - Matthew 16:26

> Therefore having overlooked the times of **ignorance**, God is now declaring to men that **all people** everywhere should **repent**.
> - Acts 17:30

Hebrews 11:6 teaches, "But without _____ it is impossible to please Him, for he who comes to God must _____ that He is, and that He is a rewarder of those who diligently _____ Him." The Bible contains everything needed, "that you may believe that Jesus is the Christ, the _____ of God, and that believing you may have _____ in His name" (John 20:31).

3. **They do not want to give up some things.**
Becoming a Christian may mean that we have to give up some things. Jesus said, "If anyone desires to come after Me, let him _____ himself, and take up his cross, and follow Me" (Matthew 16:24). What does God command all men everywhere to do? _____ (Acts 17:30). Repentance demands that we quit doing those things that are contrary to God's word and displeasing to God. Some are so wrapped up in the pleasures of sin and the things of this world that they do not want to give them up to serve God. What are some things we may have to give up to become a Christian? _____
_____
_____

The Bible says, "Do not _____ the world or the things in the world. If anyone loves the world, the love of the Father is not in him. For all that is in the world—the lust of the _____, the lust of the _____, and the _____ of life— is not of the Father but is of the world. And the world is _____ _____, and the lust of it; but he who does the will of God abides forever" (1 John 2:15-17). What did Moses choose to do when he became of age, and why? _____
_____
_____ (Hebrews 11:24-26)

4. **They love the praise of men.** Some are too concerned about what others think of them. Among the rulers many believed in Jesus, "but because of the Pharisees they did not confess Him, lest they should be put out of the synagogue" (John 12:42). What did they love more than the praise of God? _____

_____ (John 12:43). Becoming a Christian involves living a life that some think strange and speak of in evil ways (1 Peter 4:4). How would you respond to someone who thinks you are strange or weird because you do some things they don't and don't do some things they do?

_____

_____

Some do not become a Christian because they are afraid of what their friends or family may think or say. Really, the only thing that matters is what God will say at the final judgment. Will He say, "Well done, good and _____ servant...Enter into the joy of your lord" (Matthew 25:21) or "_____ from Me, you cursed, into the _____ fire prepared for the devil and his angels" (Matthew 25:41)? Will it really matter then what people thought or said about us in this life?

> In all this, they are **surprised** that you do not **run with them** into the same excesses of **dissipation**, and they **malign** you.
>
> - 1 Peter 4:4

## Don't become a Christian just because...

When one becomes a Christian, he must do so for the right reasons. Don't choose to become a Christian just because...

1. **Your parents want you to.** It is natural to want to please one's parents. We want them to be happy with us. And, if your parents are Christians, they will be pleased and happy

when you choose to become a Christian. But, don't become a Christian just because you think that's what they want you to do or just to make them happy. Becoming a Christian is your choice. You must "work out your own _____ with fear and _____" (Philippians 2:12). Become a Christian because you see the need to and want to, not because you think someone else wants you to.

Now, you finish this point. What would be some other wrong motives for becoming a Christian. Don't become a Christian just because...

_____
_____
_____
_____

## Reasons for becoming a Christian

In the remainder of this study, let's think of some spiritual reasons a person should be moved and motivated to become a Christian.

1. **The shortness and uncertainty of life.** Life is too short and uncertain to live another day outside of Jesus Christ. How much longer do you plan to live? Another year, two years, five, ten, twenty or even fifty years? The reality is that we have no guarantee that we will see the sun come up tomorrow. What does Proverbs 27:1 say? _____
_____

In Luke 12, we read about a man who had a plan "for many years" (vv. 16-21). How much longer did he live? _____
If your soul was to be required of you this night, would you be ready? Life at its longest is brief. "For what is your life? It is even a _____

> Do not **boast** about **tomorrow**, for you **do not know** what a day may bring forth.
>
> - Proverbs 27:1

that appears for a _____ _____ and then vanishes away" (James 4:14). With the help of a parent, you might perform a little experiment at home. Take a pot and put some water in it. Put it on the stove burner and turn it on. In a few minutes, you will see a steam or vapor rise. Now turn the burner off and remove the pot of water. Watch the vapor vanish away. That is your life! See how quickly it is gone?

2. **The value of the soul.** The Bible teaches that we are two men. Read 2 Corinthians 4:16 and explain. _____
   _____
   _____

   The inward man is the soul. It is God-given (Genesis 2:7; Zechariah 12:1). There is more to us than this physical body. There is a part of us that is immortal, that will survive the death of the body and outlive the world. It is the soul or spirit. Get a blank sheet of paper. Draw a circle to represent the value of your soul. How valuable did Jesus say man's soul is? _____
   _____
   Your soul is your most valuable possession!

3. **Judgment is coming.** Paul reasoned with Governor Felix about "_____ to come" and Felix was afraid (Acts 24:25). Why did Solomon say to "Fear God and keep His commandments" in Ecclesiastes 12:13? _____
   _____ (v. 14)
   Read Matthew 25:31-46 to get a glimpse of the judgment. Write down three things you learn about judgment to come from this reading.
   _____
   _____
   _____

> Therefore we do not lose heart, but though our **outer man** is **decaying**, yet our **inner man** is being **renewed** day by day.
>
> - 2 Corinthians 4:16

> And having been made **perfect**, He became to all those who **obey** Him the source of **eternal salvation**.
>
> - Hebrews 5:9

We will give account of our _____ (Matthew 12:36-37) and what we have _____ (2 Corinthians 5:10). Are you ready for the judgment day?

4. **We must obey the Lord to be saved.** Who will enter the kingdom of heaven? _____ _____ (Matthew 7:21). Jesus asked, "But why do you call Me 'Lord, Lord,' and not _____ the things which I say?" To whom is Christ the author of eternal salvation? _____ _____ (Hebrews 5:9) What will happen to those who do not obey the gospel? _____ _____ (2 Thessalonians 1:7-9) Revelation 22:14 says, "Blessed are those who _____ His commandments, that they may have right to the tree of life, and may enter through the gates into the city." If we want to go to Heaven, we must be obedient and do what God says.

5. **To have all spiritual blessings.** The blessings of God are of two kinds: physical and spiritual. God's physical blessings are such things as the sunshine and rain; these fall on all men alike (Matthew 5:45). The spiritual blessings of God are reserved for Christians. Where are these blessings found? _____ (Ephesians 1:3). Read Ephesians 1:4-14 and list some of these blessings. _____ _____ _____

   Now read Galatians 3:27 and tell how one gets into Christ to enjoy all these spiritual blessings. _____ _____

6. **To have hope.** There is nothing worse than being without hope. What was the condition of the Ephesians before they became Christians? _____ _____(Ephesians 2:12). What do you learn about hope from Romans 8:24? _____ _____ How many hopes are there? _____ (Ephesians 4:4). Who is this hope laid up for and where? _____ _____ (Colossians 1:2, 5). Christ is our hope (1 Timothy 1:1). In Him we have the "hope of eternal life" (Titus 1:2). In the storms of life, we need an anchor to keep us from drifting. What is this anchor? _____ (Hebrews 6:18-19). What a blessing to get up in the morning and know that no matter what happens, you have the hope of Heaven! And to be able to go to bed at night with the assurance that if you never wake up, all is well with your soul!

## Some questions from our study

1. Why do some not become Christians? _____
   _____
   _____

2. What would be some wrong reasons for becoming a Christian? _____
   _____
   _____

3. Give three reasons for becoming a Christian. _____
   _____
   _____

How to Become a Christian

# Understanding Sin

Understanding sin is important to becoming a Christian. Sin is what creates the need for us to become Christians. Without a proper understanding of sin, one never will recognize their need to become a Christian. Thus, we study.

## A universal problem

Sin affects all people in the world. Paul wrote concerning both Jews and Greeks, "...that they are _____ under sin" (Romans 3:9). In Romans 3:23 he said, "for _____ _____ _____ and fall short of the glory of God." Galatians 3:22 states, "But the Scripture has confined _____ under sin..." If all are under sin and all have sinned, then does sin affect you and me? _____ What two things are we doing when we say that we have no sin or have not sinned? _____ (1 John 1:8, 10) The reason this is so is because God says we have sinned. Since sin affects us all, we should be interested in learning what the Bible teaches about it.

## Is sin inherited?

Most people have been made to believe that sin is inherited, passed down from one generation to the next. It is often referred to as Adamic sin, original sin, inherited sin, or total hereditary depravity. The idea is that when an individual enters this world he is born with the guilt of his father's sin. He inherited

> **Memory Verse**
>
> For the wages of **sin** is **death**, but the **gift** of God is **eternal life** in Christ Jesus our Lord.
>
> - Romans 6:23

sin from his father and his father inherited it from his father, and this goes all the way back to Adam. The Bible does not teach this!

1. **God made man upright.** Solomon taught in the book of Ecclesiastes, "Truly, this only I have found: That God made man _____, But they have sought out many schemes" (Ecclesiastes 7:29). What does this mean?

2. **No knowledge of good and evil.** Remember when the children of Israel were made to wander in the wilderness forty years? The Lord said, "Surely not one of these men of this evil generation shall see that good land of which I swore to give to your fathers, except Caleb... and Joshua" (Deuteronomy 1:35-38). Why were their little ones and children not held responsible in the rebellion, but allowed to go in and possess the land? _____ _____ _____ (Deuteronomy 1:39) There is a time in our lives when we are totally innocent, having no knowledge of good and evil.

3. **The son does not bear the guilt of the father.** A reading of Ezekiel 18:1-20 shows that neither wickedness nor righteousness is inherited. Verse 20 says it so well: "The soul who _____ shall die. The son shall _____ bear the _____ of the father, nor the father bear the guilt of the son. The _____ of the righteous shall be upon himself, and the _____ of the wicked shall be upon himself."

4. **He who does wrong will be repaid for what he has done.** We are held individually accountable for what we have done, not for

> Moreover, your **little ones** who you said would become a prey, and your sons, who this day have **no knowledge of good or evil**, shall enter there, and I will give it to them and they shall possess it.
>
> - Deuteronomy 1:39

what our parents may or may not have done. Paul wrote, "But he who does _____ will be repaid for what _____ has done, and there is no partiality" (Colossians 3:25).

5. **Children are safe; not sinners.** When the disciples were prideful, who did Jesus call to teach them a lesson in humility? _____ (Matthew 18:1-5) He said, "unless you are converted and become as _____ _____, you will by no means enter the kingdom of heaven" (v. 3). On another occasion Jesus announced, "Let the little children come to Me, and do not forbid them; for of such is the _____ of God" (Mark 10:14).

If we are not born with the guilt of sin upon our soul, then how do we become sinners? When we learn what sin is, we will understand how it is that we become guilty of sin.

## What sin is

The word "sin" occurs 446 times in the New King James Version. Two other words that often appear as well are "iniquity" and "transgression." Exodus 34:7 uses all three words together, "iniquity, transgression and sin." We look to the Word of God to learn what sin is.

1. **Whatever is not from faith.** Paul said, "for whatever is not from faith is _____" (Romans 14:23). The word "faith" is often used in reference to the gospel (Galatians 1:23; 2:2), but in this passage it has to do with our personal faith or conscience. The context has to do with eating meat. Some had a conscience that would not allow them to eat meat. Whether

> ...who keeps lovingkindness for thousands, who forgives **iniquity, transgression** and **sin**...
>
> - Exodus 34:7

you ate meat or didn't eat meat really didn't make any difference to God. It was not wrong in and of itself. It was a matter of individual determination: "Let each be fully convinced in his own mind" (Romans 14:5). But if eating meat violated your conscience, it was a sin. So, if we violate our conscience in a matter of personal liberty, we have sinned.

2. **Knowing to do good and not doing it.** James 4:17 teaches us, "Therefore, to him who knows to do good and does not do it, to him it is _____." This is known as the sin of omission. Explain what that means. _____
_____

Give an example of knowing to do good and not doing it. _____
_____
_____

A lot of people will be lost because of not doing what they know to do, the sin of plain old neglect!

3. **Lust conceived.** James wrote, "But every man is tempted, when he is drawn away of his own _____, and enticed. Then when lust hath _____, it bringeth forth _____" (James 1:14-15). Define the word lust. _____
_____

Corruption is in the world through _____ (2 Peter 1:4). What do you learn from 1 John 2:15-17? _____
_____
_____

Read the account of the first sin in Genesis 3:1-6 and explain how lust was conceived and sin was produced. _____
_____

> For all that is in the world, the **lust of the flesh** and the **lust of the eyes** and the **boastful pride of life**, is not from the Father, but is from the **world**.
>
> - 1 John 2:16

4. **Lawlessness or transgression.** John defined sin this way: "Whoever commits sin also commits lawlessness, and sin is _____" (1 John 3:4). What is lawlessness? _____
_____
_____

   Instead of the word "lawlessness," the King James Version uses the word "transgression": sin is the transgression of the law. Picture an archer, a person who shoots with a bow and arrows, shooting at a target. If the arrow fell short of the target, the archer was said to have sinned. If the arrow went beyond the target, the archer was said to have sinned. Sin means to miss the mark. This shows two ways we sin: by falling short of what God says and by going beyond what God says. One is just as bad as the other!

> Everyone who practices **sin** also practices **lawlessness**; and sin is lawlessness.
>
> - 1 John 3:4

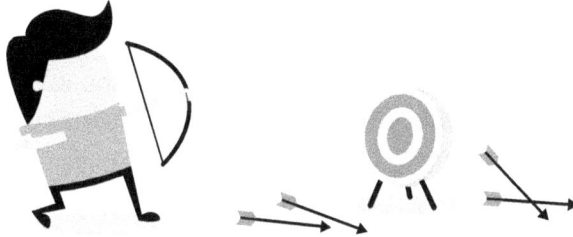

5. **All unrighteousness.** Write out the first four words of 1 John 5:17. _____
_____
_____

   Now read 1 Corinthians 6:9-11 and observe some specific acts of unrighteousness. List them. _____
_____
_____
_____

When we become involved in such things, we have _____ _____.

When we reach an age where we know the difference between good and evil and we do whatever is not from faith, don't do what we know to do, allow lust to conceive, commit lawlessness or transgression (either by going beyond or falling short of what God says) or commit acts of unrighteousness, then we become guilty of sin and will be held accountable by God for such.

## The nature of sin

Now let's think about some of the basic features or characteristics of sin.

1. **Sin is pleasurable.** Sin is attractive and appealing. It will give you a feeling of happy satisfaction and enjoyment. It is exciting and fun; it feels good! That is why there is so much of it. If there was no pleasure in sin, no one would do it. What we need to realize though is that the pleasures of sin are short-lived; they are only temporary. The feelings of pleasure are soon replaced by feelings of guilt, shame, fear, and pain that far exceed the initial pleasure produced by sin. Sin leaves scars that last a lifetime! "The way of transgressors is hard" (Proverbs 13:15, KJV). Read Hebrews 11:24-26. What choice did Moses make when he became of age? _____ _____

   Why did he make this choice? _____ _____

   We are faced with the same choice. Which will we choose?

> By faith Moses, when he had **grown up**, refused to be called the son of Pharaoh's daughter, choosing rather to endure **ill-treatment** with the people of God than to **enjoy** the passing pleasures of **sin**.
>
> - Hebrews 11:24-25

2. **Sin is deceitful.** Hebrews 3:13 says, "but exhort one another daily, while it is called 'Today,' lest any of you be hardened through the _____ of sin." Sin is misleading. It promises pleasure but delivers pain. It assures fulfillment but brings emptiness. You will find yourself believing lies like: "It's not as bad as other things;" "I'm just going to do a little bit, I'm not going to go all the way;" "I can quit anytime;" "There's no harm in it;" "Nobody will be hurt." Sin is like bait. The devil throws it out and dangles it before us, making it appear oh so irresistible. We come along and take a little nibble. He sets the hook, and he's got us! "Be _____, be _____; because your _____ the devil walks about like a roaring lion, seeking whom he may devour" (1 Peter 5:8).

3. **Sin is addictive.** Jesus taught, "Most assuredly, I say to you, whoever commits sin is a _____ of sin" (John 8:34). What does it mean to be a slave of sin? _____
   _____
   _____

   All sin is that way. It keeps you coming back for more. Decide now to break free from this ball and chain, that sin will no longer be your Master!

## What sin does

Sin brings consequences. "Do not be deceived, God is not _____; for whatever a man sows, that he will also _____" (Galatians 6:7). There are some principles we need to know about sowing and reaping that we will never change: (1) We reap what we sow; (2) We reap later than we sow; (3) We reap more than we sow.

> Do not be **deceived**, God is not **mocked**; for whatever a man **sows**, that he will also **reap**.
>
> - Galatians 6:7

> Then He will also say to those on His left, "**Depart** from Me, accursed ones, into the **eternal fire** which has been prepared for the **devil** and his **angels**."
>
> - Matthew 25:41

1. **Sin makes us of the devil.** John declared, "He who sins is of the _____, for the devil has sinned from the beginning" (1 John 3:8). We do not want to be of the devil! Consider his end. What is prepared for the devil and his angels? _____ (Matthew 25:41) Revelation 20:10 says, "they will be _____ day and night forever and ever." That's what sin will do to us!

2. **Sin separates us from God.** Sin has always brought about separation. That is what happened when Adam and Eve ate of the forbidden tree in the Garden of Eden. "The Lord God sent him _____ of the garden of Eden...So he _____ _____ the man" (Genesis 3:23-24). They were separated from God! Isaiah told the children of Israel, "Behold, the Lord's hand is not shortened, That it cannot save; Nor His ear heavy, That it cannot hear" (Isaiah 59:1). If it was not a shortened hand or heavy ear, what was the problem? _____ _____ _____ (Isaiah 59:2) The Colossians, by wicked works, were once _____ _____ (Colossians 1:21)

3. **Sin brings spiritual death.** The consequences of sin have always been death. Paul wrote the Romans, "For the wages of sin is _____, but the gift of God is eternal life in Christ Jesus our Lord" (Romans 6:23). James said, "sin, when it is full-grown, brings forth _____" (James 1:15). Physical death is the separation of the spirit from the body (James 2:26). Spiritual death is the eternal separation of the spirit from God. "These shall be punished

with everlasting destruction _____ the presence of the Lord and _____ the glory of His power" (2 Thessalonians 1:9). Sin will destroy us!

The Son of God came, "that he might _____ the works of the devil" (1 John 3:8). He is "The Lamb of God who takes away the _____ of the world!" (John 1:29). Each of us must resolve to die to sin; that is to be wholly separated from it (Romans 6:1-23). "But God be thanked that though you were slaves of sin, yet you _____ from the heart that form of doctrine to which you were delivered. And having been set _____ from sin, you became slaves of righteousness" (Romans 6:17-18). This is what we do when we become Christians. Will you be set free from sin?

## Some questions from our study

1. What are two things I do when I say I have not sinned? _____

2. Show from the Scriptures that sin is not inherited. _____

3. Using the Bible as your dictionary, define what sin is. _____

4. Give some examples of how sin is deceitful. _____

5. What does the statement, "the wages of sin is death" mean? _____

6. How do we die to sin? _____

# Lesson 4

# Hearing the Word of God

The first step in making your life right with God is hearing the word of God. All throughout the Bible, much emphasis is placed on hearing the Lord's word. The words "hear" and "hearing" occur 614 times throughout the NKJV. Let's take a look at the importance of hearing the word of God.

## Appeals to hear

Many appeals have been made down though the ages for men, women, and children to hear the word of God. Consider these examples:

1. **Moses.** He reminded the Israelites of the day when they stood before the Lord in Horeb, when the Lord said to him, "Gather the people to Me, and I will let them _____ My words" (Deuteronomy 4:10). What was the intended result of their hearing the word of God? _____
   _____
   _____

   Without hearing the Lord's word, there will be no spiritual learning! What did Moses say when he called all Israel? _____
   _____
   _____
   (Deuteronomy 5:1). Deuteronomy 6:3 says, "Therefore _____, O Israel, and be careful to observe it." The first three words of Deuteronomy 6:4 and 9:1 are "_____ _____ _____." Why was there to be a public reading of God's word before all Israel

> **Memory Verse**
>
> So then **faith** comes by **hearing**, and hearing by the **word of God**.
>
> - Romans 10:17

in their hearing every seven years? _____
_____
_____ (Deuteronomy 31:9-13)
Have you read all the word of the Lord?

2. **Joshua.** What invitation did Joshua extend unto the children of Israel, as recorded in Joshua 3:9?
_____
_____

3. **Solomon.** Numerous times the wise man appealed to hearing (Proverbs 1:8; 4:10; 5:7; 8:33; 22:17; 23:19). What will a wise man do?
_____
_____
(Proverbs 1:5) What did Solomon say to do when you go to the house of God? _____
_____
_____ (Ecclesiastes 5:1)
What closing appeal did Solomon make in Ecclesiastes 12:13? _____
_____
_____

4. **The prophets.** Micaiah said, "_____ thou therefore the _____ of the Lord" (1 Kings 22:19). What was the appeal of Elisha in 2 Kings 7:1? _____
_____

Count the number of times Isaiah called upon Judah and Jerusalem to hear the word of the Lord (Isaiah 1:2, 10; 7:13; 28:14, 23; 32:9; 33:13; 34:1; 39:5; 42:18, 23; 44:1; 47:8; 48:1, 14, 16; 51:21; 55:3; 66:5). How many? _____ "Hear the word of the Lord" (Jeremiah 2:4), "Hear this now" (Jeremiah 5:21), "Hear the word which the Lord speaks to you" (Jeremiah 10:1), "Hear and give ear" (Jeremiah 13:15) and other similar expressions are often found throughout the writings of

> **Guard** your steps as you go to the **house of God** and draw near to **listen** rather than to offer the **sacrifice of fools**; for they do not know they are doing **evil**.
>
> - Ecclesiastes 5:1

Jeremiah. Ezekiel came on the scene saying, "Ye mountains of Israel, hear the word of the Lord God" (Ezekiel 6:3). Hosea, Joel, and Amos all said, "Hear this" (Hosea 5:1; Joel 1:2; Amos 3:1). More than 50 times in the 9 chapters that make up the book of Amos reference is made to the divine source of the message with the appeal to hear the word that the Lord had spoken. Micah said, "Hear now what the Lord says" (Micah 6:1). Thus, the common theme of the prophets was for folks to hear the word of God!

5. **Jesus.** What is the Lord often reported as saying? _____
   _____ (Matthew 11:15)
   Who did Jesus say are His mother and His brothers?_____
   _____(Luke 8:21)
   Jesus taught, "_____ are those who hear the word of God and keep it!" (Luke 11:28)

6. **The Father.** What did the Father in Heaven say concerning Jesus as recorded in Matthew 17:5?
   _____
   _____

7. **Preachers in the New Testament.** How did Peter begin his sermon in Acts 2? _____
   _____ (v. 22)
   What words did they hear on that occasion?
   _____
   _____ (vv. 22-36, 38-40)
   What did those who gladly received the word do? _____ (v. 41)
   What prophecy did Peter quote in Acts 3:22-23?
   _____
   _____
   Stephen also made reference to this in Acts 7:37. Why did Cornelius summon Peter to his house

> …behold, a voice out of the cloud said, "This is My beloved **Son**, with whom I am well-pleased; **listen to Him**!"
> - Matthew 17:5

in Acts 10? _____
_____ (v. 22)
What words did he hear? _____
_____ (vv. 34-48)
How did Paul begin his message in Acts 22:1?
_____

In the context of the word of God, James said, "let every man be _____ to _____, slow to speak, slow to wrath" (James 1:19). The message of John begins with this beatitude: "Blessed is he who _____ and those who _____ the words of this prophecy, and _____ those things which are written in it" (Revelation 1:3). Seven times he says, "He who has an ear, let him hear what the Spirit says" (Revelation 2:7).

8. **The Holy Spirit.** The Hebrew writer mentioned, "Therefore, as the Holy Spirit says: 'Today, if you will hear His voice'" (Hebrews 3:7, 15; 4:7).

## Attitudes toward hearing

There are different attitudes toward hearing the word of God. Next to the passage, write the statement that expresses an attitude toward hearing the word. Circle G (for good) or B (for bad) next to the attitudes written below.

1. **1 Samuel 3:9:** _____
   _____ (G / B)

2. **2 Kings 17:14:** _____
   _____ (G / B)

3. **Psalm 85:8:** _____
   _____ (G / B)

4. **Isaiah 30:9:** _____
   _____ (G / B)

> **Blessed** is he who **reads** and those who **hear** the words of this prophecy, and **keep** those things which are written in it.
>
> - Revelation 1:3

5. Luke 5:1: _____
   _____ (G / B)

6. Luke 19:48: _____
   _____ (G / B)

7. Luke 21:38: _____
   _____ (G / B)

8. Acts 10:33: _____
   _____ (G / B)

9. Acts 13:7: _____
   _____ (G / B)

10. Acts 13:44: _____
    _____ (G / B)

Now would be a good time for you to ask yourself, "How is my attitude toward hearing the word of God? Is it good or bad?" Which of the statements above best describe your attitude?

## Warnings about hearing

Read the two passages below and write out the warnings Jesus gave concerning hearing.

1. Mark 4:24: _____
   _____
   _____

2. Luke 8:18: _____
   _____
   _____

May we heed these warnings!

## Kinds of hearers

Jesus told the Parable of the Sower who went out to sow seed. The seed is the _____ of God (Luke 8:11). The soils represent different kinds of

> Now the parable is this: the **seed** is the **word** of God.
> - Luke 8:11

hearers. Read the whole story as recorded in Mark 4:1-20. List the four different hearers.

1. _____

2. _____

3. _____

4. _____

Now, ask yourself: "Which of these am I?"

In the Sermon on the Mount, Jesus told about the wise and foolish builders (Matthew 7:24-27). These represent two different kinds of hearers. The wise man stands for one who _____ and _____, while the foolish man depicts one who hears but does _____ do.

Read James 1:22-25. He speaks of two different men. Who are they?_____
_____
_____

All of this shows that it takes more than just hearing the word; it takes obedience!

## What the word does

The importance and value of hearing the word of God is seen from all that the word does. Read the passages and write down what is accomplished by the word of God.

1. **Matthew 4:4:** _____
   _____
   _____

2. **John 5:24:** _____
   _____
   _____

> ...Man shall not live on **bread** alone, but on every **word** that proceeds out of the mouth of **God**.
>
> - Matthew 4:4

**LESSON 4** Hearing the Word of God   37

3. **John 8:31:** _____
   _____
   _____

4. **John 8:51-52:** _____
   _____
   _____

5. **John 15:3:** _____
   _____
   _____

6. **John 17:17:** _____
   _____
   _____

7. **Acts 20:32:** _____
   _____
   _____

8. **Romans 10:17:** _____
   _____
   _____

9. **2 Corinthians 5:19:** _____
   _____
   _____

10. **James 1:18:** _____
    _____
    _____

11. **James 1:21:** _____
    _____
    _____

12. **1 Peter 1:23-25:** _____
    _____
    _____

13. **1 Peter 2:2:** _____
    _____
    _____

> You are already **clean** because of the **word** which I have spoken to you.
>
> - John 15:3

The word of God has tremendous ability. In order for these benefits and blessings to be ours, we must first _____ it!

## Calling on the name of the Lord

Paul declared, "For 'whoever calls on the name of the LORD shall be saved'" (Romans 10:13). A reading of the context shows what is involved in calling on the name of the Lord. "How then shall they call on Him in whom they have not believed? And how shall they believe in Him of whom they have not _____? And how shall they _____ without a preacher?...But they have not all obeyed the gospel" (Romans 10:14, 16). So, what is the first step to calling on the name of the Lord so as to be saved? _____
_____

> How then will they **call** on Him in whom they have not **believed**? How will they believe in Him whom they have not **heard**? And how will they hear without a **preacher**?
>
> - Romans 10:14

## Cases of conversion

Every case of conversion in the book of Acts, from the Jews on Pentecost in Acts 2 to the Ephesians in Acts 19, began with individuals hearing the word of God. There are no exceptions to this rule! Look and see. Here is an example: "And many of the Corinthians, _____, believed and were baptized" (Acts 18:8).

Thus, if we want to be saved from our past sins and go to Heaven, it is absolutely necessary that we hear the word of God and be the right kind of hearer. Let's be like those in Berea who, "received the word with all readiness, and searched the scriptures daily" (Acts 17:11).

## LESSON 4 Hearing the Word of God

## Some questions from our study

1. What has been the appeal down through the ages? _____
   _____
   _____
   _____

2. What are some different attitudes one might have toward hearing the word of God? _____
   _____
   _____
   _____

3. List the two warnings Jesus gave about hearing, and tell how they relate to us today. _____
   _____
   _____
   _____

4. Make a list of different kinds of hearers. _____
   _____
   _____

5. Describe the importance and value of hearing the word of God. _____
   _____
   _____
   _____

6. Other than the case of the Corinthians mentioned in this lesson, list two cases of conversion where folks first heard the word of God. _____
   _____
   _____
   _____

# Lesson 5

# The Need for Belief

Once one has heard the word of God, he should be moved to believe. Believing is more than merely having a simple mental thought. It involves faith in God, and in His word. It includes the need for further action based upon this new feeling of belief. Believing is the motivating force which leads to righteous action. Without belief, one will not be driven to act.

## What should one believe?

The Bible has placed great importance on believing. Those wishing to be obedient to God must know what to believe. Consider the following:

1. **Believe in God.** There is a God, and such must be believed. Moses was concerned the children of Israel would not believe. God was with Moses, allowing him to do miracles, in order that the children might believe what (Exodus 4:5)? _____
   _____
   _____

   One must believe that God exists, that He always has and always will!

2. **Believe in the Son of God.** God sent His Son to live on the Earth. Those who desire to please God must believe this. Jesus said, "Therefore I said to you that you will die in your sins; for if you do not _____ that I am He, you will _____ in your _____" (John 8:24).

> **Memory Verse**
>
> But without **faith** it is impossible to please Him, for he who comes to God **must believe** that He is, and that He is a **rewarder** of those who **diligently** seek Him.
>
> - Hebrews 11:6

One must believe that Jesus is the Son of God, and that He lived and died for the good of the souls of all men and women.

3. **Believe in the word of God.** God has left His people with His word. It is the precious and divine Bible. Those eager to do right must believe each and every word in the Bible are the words of God. Read 1 Thessalonians 2:13. What was Paul thankful for in this text? _____
_____
_____

We, too, must accept the words in the Bible are the words of God.

## Some who believed

The Bible is filled with examples of those who believed. These records show great men and women who had faith in God, in Christ, and in their word. As a result, they became obedient to God and fulfilled His plan. Read the following passages. In the provided blanks, write down who believed, and what they believed.

1. **Genesis 15:4-6, Romans 4:3** _____
_____
_____

2. **Psalm 119:66** _____
_____
_____

3. **Daniel 6:23** _____
_____
_____

4. **Jonah 3:5** _____
_____
_____

> Teach me good **discernment** and **knowledge**, for I **believe** in Your commandments.
>
> - Psalm 119:66

5. John 4:42, Acts 8:12 _____
   _____
   _____

6. Acts 4:1-4 _____
   _____
   _____

7. Acts 8:13 _____
   _____
   _____

8. Acts 18:8 _____
   _____
   _____

## Some who did not believe

Just as the Bible is full of those who believed, there were also many who failed to believe, or have faith. This illustrates God will not force one to execute His will. The action of believing is left to the individual. Consider these cases:

1. **Moses and Aaron** were instructed to "_____ to the rock" in order to produce water for the thirsty children (Numbers 20:8). Yet, Moses "_____ the rock twice" (Numbers 20:11). God said, "Because you did not _____ Me…you shall not bring this assembly into the land which I have given them" (Numbers 20:12).

2. **The children of Israel** agreed with the ten spies who brought an "evil" report about the land of Canaan. Even though God had reminded them He would be with them, they "did not _____ the Lord your God" (Deuteronomy 1:32).

> Even Simon himself **believed**; and after being **baptized**, he continued on with Philip, and as he observed **signs** and great **miracles** taking place, he was constantly **amazed**.
>
> - Acts 8:13

> And behold, you shall be **silent** and unable to speak until the day when these things take place, because you did not **believe** my words, which will be **fulfilled** in their proper time.
> - Luke 1:20

3. **The Queen of Sheba** heard about the wisdom of Solomon. However, she required evidence of it. She admitted, "However, I did not _____ the words until I came and saw with my own _____" (1 Kings 10:7).

4. **Zacharias** and his wife Elizabeth longed for a child of their own. Elizabeth was unable to have children, and they were both advanced in years. Nevertheless, the angel Gabriel announced to Zacharias he would have a son (Luke 1:13). Later, it is recorded Zacharias "did not _____" the words of the angel (Luke 1:20).

5. **Thomas** was not with the apostles when Jesus appeared to them after having been raised from the dead. His statement was, "Unless I _____ in His hands the print of the nails, and _____ my finger into the print of the nails, and put my hand into His side, I will not _____" (John 20:25).

It should be noticed the various reasons why some did not believe. Some lost faith as circumstances became difficult (Moses and Aaron). Others lacked belief due to the lies of others (children of Israel). Several refused to believe until they had visual evidence (Queen of Sheba and Thomas). One refused to have faith simply because the news was just too hard to believe (Zacharias).

We must overcome any obstacle which would cause us not to believe. We must develop a strong and vibrant faith.

## Benefits of believing

Great rewards come to those who believe, and have faith in God. Study the following texts, and make a note of the blessings of the believer.

**LESSON 5** The Need for Belief  45

1. 2 Chronicles 20:20 _____
   _____
   _____

2. John 3:16 _____
   _____
   _____

3. John 6:35 _____
   _____
   _____

4. John 11:25, 1 Timothy 1:16 _____
   _____
   _____

5. Acts 10:43 _____
   _____
   _____

6. Romans 4:22-24 _____
   _____
   _____

Today, those who display the same type of belief and faith these did—can expect to receive the same amazing benefits!

## Results of disbelief

We must guard against unbelief. A lack of faith will lead to tragic consequences. Reflect upon the following results of disbelief:

1. **The anger of God.** When relating the events concerning Moses striking the rock, the Psalmist pointed out this event caused the Lord to be "_____" (Psalm 78:21). In the same verse, we see a "_____ was kindled" and that God's "_____ also came up."

> Jesus said to them, "I am the **bread of life**; he who comes to Me will not **hunger**, and he who **believes** in Me will never **thirst**."
>
> - John 6:35

2. **Condemnation.** As Jesus was offering a final plea to His disciples, He said, "He who believes and is baptized will be saved; but he who does not _____ will be _____" (Mark 16:16).

3. **Impossibility of pleasing God.** The Hebrew writer penned, "But without _____ it is _____ to please Him, for he who comes to God must _____ that He is, and that He is a rewarder of those who diligently seek Him" (Hebrews 11:6).

Nobody can spiritually afford to arouse God's anger, or remain in sin. The cost is too great to bear!

## Believing is doing

Believing is not merely a mental process. It is not a plain matter of simply saying, "I believe." Such is a good start. Still, we must understand Bible belief leads to the taking of action.

Hebrews 11, the faith "hall of fame," helps us to clearly see this to be true. How many times does "by faith" appear in this chapter? _____ This implies action! It indicates something was done because of belief. What was done "by faith" in the following verses?

1. Verse 4 _____

2. Verse 5 _____

3. Verse 8 _____

> By **faith** Abraham, when he was called, **obeyed** by **going** out to a place which he was to receive for an **inheritance**; and he went out, **not knowing** where he was going.
> - Hebrews 11:8

4. Verse 17 _____
   _____
   _____

5. Verse 24 & 27 _____
   _____
   _____

6. Verse 30 _____
   _____
   _____

7. Verse 31 _____
   _____
   _____

## Belief in your life

Those who were converted to the Lord in the Bible believed after having heard the word preached. They were not forced to believe, but made the choice to do so.

Just the same, those who desire to be saved today must make the choice to believe. It is the work of God that you believe in Him who was sent (John 6:29). Those who believe even though they have not seen are blessed (John 20:29).

If we long for our sins to be removed, and have a relationship with God, we must believe with all of our heart (Acts 8:37), and let that belief move us to do God's will. Will you?

...**Blessed** are they who **did not see**, and yet **believed**.

- John 20:29

## Some questions from our study

1. What are some things one needs to believe?
   _____
   _____
   _____

## How to Become a Christian

2. Give three examples of those who believed. _____
   _____
   _____

3. Who were some who did not believe? _____
   _____
   _____

4. What sort of blessings can believers expect to receive? _____
   _____
   _____

5. Explain the dangers of disbelieving. _____
   _____
   _____

6. Describe in your own words what "by faith" means. _____
   _____
   _____

# The Importance of Repentance

## Lesson 6

As one considers becoming a Christian, and has heard the word of God and believes what it teaches, he will be motivated to repent. In its most basic form, repentance simply means change. This type of action is something God has always required of those wishing to be His people. Because all men sin (Romans 3:23), all men need to repent, or change. This is a quality of the obedient.

## What does the word "repent" mean?

In the box below, please write down in your own words what you feel it means to repent.

Simply put, the word repent means to "change one's mind or purpose." It involves a portion of regret or sorrow with regard to previous decisions or actions. In fact, repenting does not always involve sinful action. The Bible indicates there were several times when God repented. This, in no way, implies God had sinned. Rather, it means God had changed His mind. Look up the following passages,

### Memory Verse

The Lord is not **slack** concerning His **promise**, as some count slackness, but is **longsuffering** toward us, not willing that any should **perish** but that all should come to **repentance**.

- 2 Peter 3:9

> The Lord was **sorry** that He had made man on the earth, and He was **grieved** in His heart.
> - Genesis 6:6

and in the provided blank write down the word(s) which indicate a change of mind.

1. **Genesis 6:6** _____
   _____

2. **Exodus 32:14** _____
   _____

3. **Judges 2:18** _____
   _____

4. **1 Samuel 15:35** _____
   _____

5. **Jonah 3:10** _____
   _____

These verses help us understand the idea of repentance. They help show that in order to please God and comply with His commands, change is necessary.

## Bible calls for repentance

The word of God is overflowing with God and His workers calling for repentance. These appeals were made in order to persuade men to turn away from sin to God. Think about the following examples:

1. John the Baptist was saying "_____, for the kingdom of heaven is at hand" (Matthew 3:2).

2. Jesus began to teach men needed to "_____, for the kingdom of heaven is at hand" (Matthew 4:17).

3. Jesus sent his disciples on the 'Limited Commission.' As part of it "they went out and _____ that people should _____" (Mark 6:12).

4. Near the conclusion of the first recorded gospel lesson, Peter said, "_____, and let every one of you be baptized in the name of Jesus Christ for the remission of _____; and you shall receive the _____ of the Holy Spirit" (Acts 2:38).

5. Peter and John commanded those at the temple to "_____ therefore and be converted, that your _____ may be blotted out" (Acts 3:19).

6. Upon sinning, Simon the Sorcerer was told to "_____ therefore of this your wickedness, and pray God if perhaps the thought of your heart may be _____ you" (Acts 8:22).

7. Paul ended his powerful sermon on Mars Hill by calling upon "_____ men everywhere to _____" (Acts 17:30).

The appeals made then are still being made today. The one wishing to become a Christian must fulfill the demand for change.

## Requirements of Bible repentance

Just as it is with almost anything, there are requirements which must be met in order to make repentance effective. Study the following conditions.

1. **Godly sorrow.** Paul penned, "For _____ sorrow produces _____ leading to salvation, not to be regretted; but the sorrow of the world produces death" (2 Corinthians 7:10). When one has godly sorrow, he is sorry for transgressing God's law. Worldy sorrow indicates one is sorry he got caught. This is why repentance is often paired with those sitting

> Therefore **repent** and **return**, so that your **sins** may be **wiped away**, in order that times of **refreshing** may come from the presence of the Lord.
>
> - Acts 3:19

in "sackcloth and _____," a sure sign of sorrow (Luke 10:13, Matthew 11:21).

2. **Conversion.** Peter demanded the people at the temple "Repent therefore and be _____" (Acts 3:19). Conversion is often confused with repentance, but they are unique activities. While repentance indicates a change of heart, conversion stresses the need for action and compliance. For instance, Jesus taught men need to be converted like little children (Matthew 18:3). This necessitates action on the part of the individual. Those repenting must comply and act in such a way which is consistent with God's word.

3. **A turning.** When Paul and Barnabas were being treated like "gods," they insisted the people should stop and that they "should turn _____ these _____ things _____ the living _____, who made the heaven, the earth, the sea, and all things that are in them" (Acts 14:15). Repentance means one will "turn his back" on a life of sin, and turn "around" to please God. Without this turning, change cannot occur. This same situation may be found when reading Acts 26:20.

4. **Zeal.** When Jesus was concluding his remarks to the seven Asian Minor churches, he declared, "As many as I love, I rebuke and chasten. Therefore be _____ and _____" (Revelation 3:19). Those who need to repent should feel an urgency to do so! There is no need for waiting, or for procrastinating. Many who wait until a later date to obey often never find the time.

> Those whom I **love**, I **reprove** and **discipline**; therefore be **zealous** and **repent**.
>
> - Revelation 3:19

5. **Follow-up action.** The lamenting prophet recorded, "_____ now everyone of his evil way and his evil doings, and _____ in the land that the LORD has given to you and your fathers forever and ever" (Jeremiah 25:5). The word "and" in this text is important. It binds together two actions. First repent, and then do or put something proper in its place. It is not enough to simply stop doing something. Another good, godly action must take its place. This is why New Testament speakers often said show fruits of repentance (Matthew 3:8, Luke 3:8). Read Matthew 27:3-5. Judas was remorseful. Did he take proper follow-up action? _____

## What if one refuses to repent?

Multitudes of folks have refused to change over the span of time. Many still do. Though this is true, those refusing to repent must understand there are very severe and stiff consequences which accompany the refusal. Study the following passages and make a note of the penalty or penalties which come as a result of one refusing to repent.

1. **Hosea 11:1-5** _____

2. **Matthew 11:20-24** _____

3. **Luke 13:3, 5** _____

> Therefore **repent** and **return**, so that your **sins** may be **wiped away**, in order that times of **refreshing** may come from the presence of the Lord.
>
> - Acts 3:19

> Therefore **repent**; or else I am coming to you **quickly**, and I will make **war** against them with the **sword** of My mouth.
>
> - Revelation 2:16

4. Revelation 2:16 _____
   _____
   _____

5. Revelation 2:21-22 _____
   _____
   _____

The results of non-repentance are drastic. They will cost one an eternal home with God and the faithful.

## Repentance in its truest form

When understood in its fullest and most complete form, repentance is a two-part action. It is (1) A change of heart or mind which leads to (2) A change of conduct or behavior. Repentance has not truly been achieved until both parts have been completed. The Bible helps us see this picture by noting those who turned from one thing to another. Based on the following verses, fill in the provided blanks.

1. The Israelites turned from serving _____ (Deuteronomy 4:28) to serving the Lord your _____ (Deuteronomy 4:30).

2. Israel had been without the true _____, without a teaching _____ and without _____ (2 Chronicles 15:3). Yet, they turned to the Lord _____ in their trouble (2 Chronicles 15:4).

3. Paul wrote of those who "turned to _____ from _____ to serve the living and true _____" (1 Thessalonians 1:9).

## Examples of repentance

There are several outstanding illustrations of repenting, or changing in the Bible. These serve as excellent patterns to follow.

1. The people of Nineveh were set to be destroyed by God. Jonah was instructed to go and preach to them. Eventually, he did. What did the people of Nineveh do which indicated they were repenting of their sin (Jonah 3:5-6)?

   _____
   _____

   Jonah 3:10 does indeed relate the people of Nineveh had "_____ from their evil _____." Jesus spoke of this event (Matthew 12:41; Luke 11:32).

2. Read Matthew 21:28-31. What did the first son do? _____
   _____

3. Read Luke 15:11-21. What statement in verse 17 indicates he had hit "rock bottom" and was ready to repent? _____
   _____
   _____

   Based upon his change of heart, what plans did he make? _____
   _____

## Repentance in your life

Converts in the Bible repented as a result of hearing and believing the precious word of God. Today, God expects the very same of those who desire to be Christians.

Repentance comes not as a result of some miraculous event in one's life (Luke 16:30-31). It arises from deep within the heart of one who desires life (Acts 11:18), and who longs to be a recipient of the goodness of God (Romans 2:4). May each reader of this material have such desires!

…God has granted to the Gentiles also the **repentance** that leads to **life**.

- Acts 11:18

## Some questions from our study

1. What is a simple definition of the word repent? _____
   _____
   _____

2. Name three Bible teachers who called for repentance. _____
   _____

3. What were the five listed requirements of Bible repentance?
   _____
   _____
   _____
   _____
   _____

4. What dangers exist to those unwilling to repent? _____
   _____
   _____

# The Call for Confession

When one expresses interest in becoming a Christian, he will be persuaded to confess. This is the Biblical and natural step one takes after hearing and believing the word of God, and after being willing to repent, or change. The Bible contains abundant information concerning this subject.

## How is confession defined?

There are several different ways confession can be described. Consider the following ways.

1. **To declare openly.** When one feels the obligation to openly, or publicly proclaim something, it amounts to a confession. For instance, when John the Baptist was preparing the way for the Lord, many wondered who he was, and even asked him (John 1:19). His answer included a public declaration, or confession. John wrote "He _____, and did not deny, but confessed, 'I am _____ the _____'" (John 1:20).

2. **To freely and orally state an inward conviction.** At times, one has such a strong belief welling up inside him, the only thing he can do is tell others about it. To suppress such a feeling would be to contradict self. This was true of Abraham and the early followers of God who "_____ they were strangers and _____ on the earth" (Hebrews 11:13).

> **Memory Verse**
>
> Whoever **confesses** that **Jesus** is the Son of **God**, God **abides** in him, and he in God
>
> - 1 John 4:15

> If we **confess** our sins, He is faithful and just to **forgive** us our sins and to **cleanse** us from all unrighteousness.
> - 1 John 1:9

3. **To admit something.** Often men are found to be wrong on a certain subject. They have learned that a previous belief or conviction was false. Consequently, in order to do right, admission, or confession must be made. Christians occasionally find themselves in this state. John wrote "If we _____ our sins, He is faithful and just to forgive us our sins and to cleanse us from all unrighteousness" (1 John 1:9).

## Confession in God's scheme of redemption

This entire workbook is designed to help one see God's plan for them, to understand God has provided a pathway to salvation. Confession is a part of it. This confession is one which shows allegiance to Christ as one's Master and Lord. This confession is not one of sin, but of someone who is acknowledging that Jesus Christ is the Son of God.

There is an abundance of New Testament passages which prove this to be true. Think about the following:

1. Jesus did not depart this earth without leaving instructions for those who wish to be followers of Him. He said "Therefore whoever _____ Me before men, him I will also _____ before My Father who is in heaven" (Matthew 10:32). Luke recorded the same by writing, "Also I say to you, whoever _____ Me before men, him the Son of Man also will _____ before the angels of God" (Luke 12:8).

2. John penned, "Every spirit that _____ that Jesus Christ has _____ in the flesh is of _____" (1 John 4:2).

3. Once one has made this good confession, he is to maintain it. What do Hebrews 4:14 and Hebrews 10:23 say we should do with our confession? _____
_____
_____

That is, an individual who has confessed Jesus as the Son of God continues to believe and acknowledge it for the rest of his life.

## The consequences of not confessing Jesus

Though the Bible clearly called for confession, many refused to do so. Even today, many decline the offer to acknowledge Jesus. There are penalties associated with non-confession. Read the following verses. Please make a note of what one can expect by not confessing Jesus.

1. **Matthew 10:33** _____
_____

2. **1 John 2:22-23** _____
_____

3. **1 John 4:3** _____
_____

4. **2 John 7** _____
_____

It is also important to recognize why some in the Bible refused to confess Jesus. Read John 12:42-43 and answer the following questions:

> Let us **hold fast** the **confession** of our hope without **wavering**, for He who promised is **faithful**.
>
> - Hebrews 10:23

1. Who believed in Jesus? _____
   _____

2. What did they not do because of the Pharisees?
   _____
   _____

3. What were they afraid of if they did confess?
   _____
   _____

4. Ultimately, these men had a greater love for what? _____
   _____

Great danger awaits those who are unwilling to confess Jesus as the Son of God. This danger is especially serious to the one who falls in love with the world (1 John 2:15-17). Make a promise not to be among them!

> Do not **love** the **world** nor the things in the world. If anyone loves the world, the love of the **Father** is not in him.
> - 1 John 2:15

## The demands of confession

Confession comes with certain Biblical demands. These requirements must be met in order for the confession to be effective. Study the following Scriptures to see these necessities:

1. **Must be made with the mouth.** Paul wrote, "that if you _____ with your _____ the Lord Jesus and believe in your heart that God has raised Him from the dead, you will be saved. For with the heart one believes unto righteousness, and with the _____ confession is made unto _____" (Romans 10:9-10). This simply means one who desires to do right must orally confess.

2. **Must be of the Son of God.** As noted earlier, many have confessed many different things.

But the confession which is part of God's plan for salvation is with regard to His Son. John alerted us to this fact when writing, "Whoever _____ that Jesus is the _____ of _____, God abides in him, and he in God" (1 John 4:15).

3. **Must be followed by obedience.** The Lord asked, "But _____ do you call Me 'Lord, Lord,' and not _____ the things which I say" (Luke 6:46)? Since confession involves one pledging allegiance to Christ as Lord, confession involves obeying the Lord. Acknowledging Jesus as the Son of God requires my obedience to Him.

> Why do you call Me, "**Lord, Lord**," and do not **do** what I **say**?
> - Luke 6:46

## Examining the Ethiopian eunuch's confession

The very best example of this confession is that of the Ethiopian eunuch. His experience is related in Acts 8:26-40. As Philip preached "Jesus" to him (Acts 8:35), the eunuch began to understand his responsibility to the Lord. When asked about being baptized, what did Philip say to the eunuch in Acts 8:37? _____
_____
_____

When the eunuch heard this, his response was: "I _____ that Jesus Christ is the _____ of _____."

Think about the eunuch's confession in terms of the individual words. On the next page, circle the appropriate response to the statement. (T) is true and (F) is false.

> And Philip said, "If you **believe** with all your **heart**, you may." And he answered and said, "I **believe** that **Jesus Christ** is the **Son of God**."
>
> - Acts 8:37

### The eunuch's confession (Acts 8:37)

**T or F** It would be acceptable for Philip to make the confession for the eunuch.

**T or F** In order to confess Jesus, the eunuch must have believed with all of his heart.

**T or F** The eunuch nodded his head to indicate he believed that Jesus was the Son of God.

**T or F** It would have been okay for Philip to baptize the eunuch without him confessing his faith in Jesus.

**T or F** The eunuch, in his confession, admitted he fully believed Jesus was the Son of God.

From this exercise, we glean some very important reminders concerning confession.

1. You cannot make it for someone else, nor can any other individual make it for you.

2. You must have complete faith in this statement. It cannot be half-hearted or counterfeit. You fully and completely believe.

3. You understand that Jesus Christ left Heaven (Philippians 2:1-8) and lived on earth. You understand He died a cruel death through no fault of His own. You recognize He rose from the dead after having been in the grave three days.

4. You have no doubt in this statement whatsoever. There is no mental hesitation or reservation on your part.

5. You altogether, and without reluctance, believe Jesus is the Son of God. You identify Him not as a prophet from God or a teacher from the Father, but as who He is—the Son

of the Living God. You confess the same as Peter, when he said, "You are the _____, the _____ of the living _____" (Matthew 16:16).

## Confession in your life

Laid upon you is the responsibility and privilege of confessing Jesus as the Son of God. God requires our admittance of this, and our allegiance to it.

One day, every tongue will confess that Jesus Christ is Lord (Philippians 2:11). Sadly, for many it will be too late. Let this not be said of you. Make a determination to confess Jesus in your life!

## Some questions from our study

1. What are three ways confession can be defined? _____
   _____
   _____
   _____

2. In God's plan of salvation, what is one confessing? _____
   _____

3. List two consequences of not confessing. _____
   _____
   _____

4. What were the three demands of Bible confession? _____
   _____
   _____
   _____

# Lesson 8

# The Necessity of Baptism

The next step in becoming a Christian is to be baptized. Many have been made to believe that baptism is not essential to salvation. Let's look to the Bible to find out whether or not baptism is necessary to be saved.

## Baptism saves

The Lord taught, "He who believes and is _____ will be _____; but he who does not believe will be condemned" (Mark 16:16). Notice the two "he's". Who is the "he" that will be saved? _____
_____

Now observe the order of the verse. Where did the Lord put salvation: before or after baptism? _____

What is the meaning and significance of the word "and" as used here? _____
_____

Circle the correct statement: "He who believes and is baptized will be saved" or "He who believes and is not baptized will be saved." Can you think of a statement that is parallel to the Lord's statement in Mark 16:16? _____
_____

Peter declared, "There is also an antitype which now _____ us—_____" (1 Peter 3:21).

Circle the statement that is correct: "There is also an antitype which now saves us—baptism" or "There is also an antitype which does not save us—baptism."

> **Memory Verse**
>
> He who **believes** and is **baptized** will be **saved**; but he who does **not believe** will be **condemned**.
>
> - Mark 16:16

Just as surely as Noah and his family were "saved through water" (1 Peter 3:20), the Bible teaches that we are saved by baptism.

## Baptism is for the remission of sins

Peter said, "Repent, and let every one of you be _____ in the name of Jesus Christ _____ the _____ of _____" (Acts 2:38). What is "the remission of sins"? _____
_____

A lot hinges on the word "for". What does it mean?
_____
_____

Notice the word "and." What is its importance?
_____
_____

Did the Lord ever use this same expression, "for the remission of sins"? If so, where and what application can be made of it here? _____
_____
_____

## Baptism is included in every case of New Testament conversion

Without exception, in every case where men and women were converted in New Testament days, they were baptized. Notice that such was the case:

Acts 2:41_____

Acts 8:12_____

Acts 8:13_____

Acts 8:38 _____

Acts 9:18_____

> So then, those who had **received** his word were **baptized**; and that day there were **added** about **three thousand souls**.
>
> - Acts 2:41

**LESSON 8** The Necessity of Baptism

Acts 10:48 _____

Acts 16:15 _____

Acts 16:33 _____

Acts 18:8 _____

Acts 19:5 _____

If baptism is not a necessity, when then were all these baptized? And notice when they were baptized—the same hour (Acts 16:33), the same day (Acts 2:41). Why be baptized the same hour, the same day? _____ _____ (Proverbs 27:1)

## Baptism is a must

The Lord told Saul, "Arise and go into the city, and you will be told what you _____ do" (Acts 9:6). Define the word "must." _____ _____

Fill in the blank: If a thing is a must, then it is _____! Now the question is: What was Saul told to do? _____ _____ _____ (Acts 22:16)

## Baptism is commanded

In the case of the Gentiles, it is recorded of Peter, "And he _____ them to be _____ in the name of the Lord" (Acts 10:48). When one says baptism is not necessary to salvation, what is he really saying? _____ _____

Baptism is an act of obedience required by the Lord to be saved (Hebrews 5:9).

> Do not **boast** about **tomorrow**, for you **do not know** what a **day** may bring forth.
>
> - Proverbs 27:1

## Baptism washes away sins

Ananias said unto Saul, "And now why are you waiting? Arise and be _____, and _____ _____ _____ _____."
(Acts 22:16). Is it necessary for one to have his sins washed away? _____ If so, then baptism is (you finish the sentence) _____

## Baptism is involved in calling on the name of the Lord

What promise was made concerning "Whoever calls on the name of the Lord" (Joel 2:28-32; Acts 2:16-21)? _____

Read Romans 10:13-17 and explain how one calls on the name of the Lord. _____
_____

Now back to Ananias' statement to Saul in Acts 22:16. "Arise and be _____...
_____ ____ _____ _____ ____ _____ _____." Can one be saved without calling on the name of the Lord? _____ If not, then what must he to do to be saved?_____

## Baptism puts one into the death of Christ

List eight things the blood of Christ does:
_____ (Matthew 26:28)
_____ (Romans 5:9)
_____ (Ephesians 1:7)
_____ (Ephesians 2:13)
_____ (Colossians 1:20)
_____ (Hebrews 9:14)
_____ (Hebrews 10:29)
_____ (Revelation 1:5)

The blood of Christ and the death of Christ go together as the Lord shed His blood in His death (John 19:33-34). Now Read Romans 6:3-4 to learn

> And it will come about that whoever **calls** on the name of the **Lord** will be **delivered**...
>
> - Joel 2:32

how one reaches the death of Christ and comes into contact with the blood of Christ: "Or do you not know that as many of us as were baptized into Christ were _____ into His _____? Therefore we were buried with Him through _____ into _____: that just as Christ was raised from the dead by the glory of the Father, even so we also should walk in newness of life" (Romans 6:3-4). How does Romans 6:17-18 tie in with this teaching? _____
_____

## Baptism puts one into the one body

There is _____ body (Ephesians 4:4), which is the _____ (Ephesians 1:22-23; Colossians 1:18, 24). List three things that are in the one body:
_____ (Colossians 3:15)
_____ (Ephesians 2:16)
_____ (Ephesians 5:23; Acts 2:47)
How does one enter the one body? _____
_____ (1 Corinthians 12:13)

## Baptism puts one into Christ

There are many advantages of being in Christ. This is where _____ (Romans 3:24), all _____ _____ (Ephesians 1:3), _____ (2 Timothy 2:10), and the hope and promise of _____ _____ (Titus 1:2; 1 John 2:25) are all found! Read Galatians 3:27 and tell how one gets into Christ. _____
_____

Surely you can see from this simple study that one must be baptized as the Bible teaches in order to be saved. "And now why are you waiting? Arise and be baptized, and wash away your sins, calling on the name of the Lord" (Acts 22:16).

> For by one Spirit we were all **baptized** into one **body**, whether **Jews** or **Greeks**, whether **slaves** or **free**, and we were all made to **drink** of one **Spirit**.
>
> - 1 Corinthians 12:13

## Some questions from our study

1. Write out and memorize Mark 16:16. _____
   _____
   _____
   _____

2. How are we saved like Noah? _____
   _____
   _____

3. What does it mean that baptism is for the remission of sins? _____
   _____
   _____

4. Give three examples of people in the New Testament who were baptized. _____
   _____
   _____

5. When were folks in New Testament days baptized? _____
   _____

6. What is involved in calling on the name of the Lord? _____
   _____

7. What are the three things baptism brings us into? _____
   _____
   _____
   _____

# Lesson 9

# The Action of Baptism

The Lord commanded, "Go therefore and make disciples of all the nations, baptizing them" (Matthew 28:19). There is disagreement in the religious world as to what is meant by "baptizing them." Is Bible baptism a sprinkling or pouring of water upon a person or immersion of the whole person in water? Does it really make any difference?

## The creeds of men

"United Methodists may baptize by any of the modes used by Christians. Candidates or their parents have the choice of sprinkling, pouring, or immersion; and pastors and congregations should be prepared to honor requests for baptism in any of these modes. Each mode brings out part of the rich and diverse symbolism given to baptism by the Bible" (*The United Methodist Book of Worship*, Copyright 1992, The United Methodist Publishing House). "What is the meaning of the word 'baptize'? 'Baptize' means to apply water by washing, pouring, sprinkling, or immersing" (*Luther's Small Catechism*, p. 170). "Dipping of the person into the water is not necessary; but baptism is rightly administered by pouring or sprinkling water upon the person" (*The Confession of Faith of the Presbyterian Church*, p. 161). "Baptism is performed in the most expressive way by triple immersion in the baptismal water. However, from ancient times it has also been able to be conferred by pouring the water three times over the candidate's head"

## Memory Verse

**Buried** with Him in **baptism**, in which you also were **raised** with Him through **faith** in the working of **God**, who raised Him from the **dead**.

- Colossians 2:12

(*Catechism of the Catholic Church*, p. 317). "What is Christian baptism?...Baptists answer the question by saying that baptism is the immersion, dipping, or burying in water, of a professed believer in Christ... Neither sprinkling a person with water, nor pouring water upon him can by any possibility be Christian baptism" (*The Standard Manual for Baptist Churches*, pp. 80-81).

### Religious leaders

Interestingly, some leaders of churches that practice sprinkling or pouring admit Bible baptism is immersion. Consider some examples:

Adam Clark (Methodist): "Alluding to the immersion practiced in the case of adults, wherein the person appeared to be buried under the water, as Christ was buried in the heart of the earth. His rising again the third day, and their emerging from the water, was an emblem of the resurrection of the body" (Commentary on Colossians 2:12).

Mosheim (Lutheran): "The sacrament of baptism was administered in this century (the first) without the public assemblies, in places appointed and prepared for that purpose, and was performed by an immersion of the whole body in the baptismal font" (*Mosheim's Church History*, Vol. 1, p. 343).

John Calvin (Presbyterianism): "The very word 'baptize,' however, signifies immerse, and it is certain that immersion was the practice of the ancient church" (*Institutes*, Vol. 3, p. 343).

Brenner (Roman Catholic): "Thirteen hundred years was baptism generally and regularly an immersion of the person under water, and only in extraordinary cases a sprinkling or pouring with water; the latter was, moreover, disputed as a

> The very word **baptize**, however, signifies **immerse**, and it is **certain** that **immersion** was the practice of the **ancient church**.
> 
> - John Calvin, *Institutes*

mode of baptism, nay, even forbidden" (*A Handbook on Christian Baptism*, Richard Ingham, p. 159).

## English dictionaries

An English dictionary may define baptism as follows: "the religious rite of sprinkling water onto a person's forehead or of immersion in water, symbolizing purification or regeneration and admission to the Christian Church" (*New Oxford American Dictionary*). What is the problem with consulting a modern English dictionary to define Bible words? _____
_____
_____

## Greek definitions

The Greek word for baptism is *baptisma* and for baptize is *baptizo*. These are not translations, but are transliterations from the Greek language into the English language. How these words are defined:

"*Baptisma*—baptism, consisting of the processes of immersion, submersion, and emergence (from *bapto*, to dip)" (*Vine's Expository Dictionary of New Testament Words*, pp. 96-97).

"*Baptizo*—to baptize, primarily a frequentative form of *bapto*, to dip, was used among the Greeks to signify the dyeing of a garment, or the drawing of water by dipping a vessel into another, etc." (Ibid.).

There are Greek words for sprinkle (*rantizo*) and pour (*cheo*). These words were not used, however. The Lord and His apostles always and only used a word that means immersion and never means sprinkling or pouring in speaking of this action required to become a Christian!

> *Baptisma*: consisting of the processes of **immersion**, **submersion**, and **emergence**
>
> - *Vine's Expository Dictionary of New Testament Words*

## The scriptures

Examples of baptism in the Scriptures demonstrate immersion; not sprinkling or pouring.

Baptism of Jesus (Matthew 3:13, 16; Mark 1:9-10).
_____
_____
_____

Baptism of the Ethiopian (Acts 8:36, 38-39).
_____
_____
_____

Words used in connection with baptism in the Scriptures affirm the action is immersion; not sprinkling or pouring.

John 3:23 _____
_____

Romans 6:4-5 _____
_____

Colossians 2:12 _____
_____

Now, make a list of things the action of Bible baptism requires. _____
_____
_____

There is no example anywhere in the New Testament where anyone under any circumstance ever had water sprinkled or poured upon them for any purpose whatsoever. If so, where is the Scripture?_____

## History of sprinkling and pouring

The first case of sprinkling was Novation in 250 A.D. The Roman Catholic Church did not

> John also was **baptizing** in Aenon near Salim, because there was **much water** there; and people were coming and were being **baptized**.
>
> - John 3:23

officially substitute sprinkling for immersion until the council of Ravenna in 1311 A.D. Protestant denominationalism has inherited it from Roman Catholicism.

## Answering objections to immersion

"Acts 8:26 says, 'Gaza, which is desert.' Therefore, there could have been no water there." _____
_____
_____

"The eunuch may have pulled out a water bag or jug from underneath the seat of his chariot and said, 'See, here is water; what doth hinder me to be baptized?'" _____
_____
_____

"If sprinkling and pouring are wrong, why doesn't the Bible say not to do it that way?" _____
_____
_____

"What about a person who is in such a physical condition that he/she can't be immersed in water; the doctors forbid it?" _____
_____
_____

Clearly, the action of Bible baptism is immersion; not sprinkling or pouring. When you are baptized, you will come unto a certain water, go down into the water, be baptized and come up out of the water! Do not accept sprinkling or pouring of water upon you as a substitute for Bible teaching on baptism!

> Therefore we have been **buried** with Him through **baptism** into **death**, so that as Christ was **raised** from the dead through the glory of the Father, so we too might walk in **newness** of life.
>
> - Romans 6:4

## Some questions from our study

1. What do the creeds of men say about the action of baptism? _____
   _____
   _____

2. How does a modern dictionary define baptism? _____
   _____
   _____

3. What is the meaning of the word "baptism" in the original language?
   _____
   _____

4. List some Scriptures which clearly show the action of baptism is burial or immersion in water. _____
   _____
   _____

5. What does the action of baptism in the Bible require? _____
   _____
   _____

# Why Do Some Wait?

It is crucial one sees the need for obedience to the Lord, and to His plan for saving them. At times though, some delay obedience. There is great danger in putting off obedience. Man has been doing such things for as long as he has existed. Whatever reason one has for not being baptized and being a worker for the Lord, it must be overcome. Why do some put off being baptized into Christ and obeying him, putting self aside? Consider.

## Some believe baptism is not necessary

Some, after having read the word of God, and after having been clearly taught, still believe baptism is not necessary to be saved. Carefully study the following and note what baptism accomplishes.

1. Jesus said, "He who believes and is _____ will be _____; but he who does not believe will be condemned" (Mark 16:16). Two actions are required for salvation in this verse, belief and baptism. Accepting one but not the other fails to produce deliverance from sin.

2. Peter penned, "There is also an antitype which now _____ us — _____ (not the removal of the filth of the flesh, but the answer of a good conscience toward God), through the resurrection of Jesus Christ" (1 Peter 3:21). Baptism is not for the purpose of removing physical filth, but spiritual.

**Memory Verse**

And now why are you **waiting**? Arise and be **baptized**, and wash away your **sins**, **calling** on the name of the **Lord**.

- Acts 22:16

3. Saul was told, "_____ and be _____, and wash away your _____" (Acts 22:16). Man must take action in order for his sins to be removed.

Notice the connection in these verses between baptism and salvation, or the washing away of sin. Neither can be accomplished without it.

## Some believe they are already saved

Many have been immersed in water before, but they were not baptized "in the name of the Lord Jesus" (Acts 19:5). Often, this occurred when water was poured or sprinkled on an individual when they were just an infant.

Read Acts 19:1-5. Answer the following questions.

1. What original question did Paul ask the men in Ephesus? _____
   _____

2. These men had only been baptized by which baptism? _____

3. Did John's baptism involve repentance?
   _____

4. After Paul had taught them about Jesus, and the baptism He commanded (Matthew 28:18-20), what did these men do? _____
   _____

One must have a very clear understanding of what he is doing when being baptized. This responsibility falls upon both the student and the teacher.

Being "baptized" as an infant, or being baptized because one felt pressured to do so, or being baptized because other friends were doing it is not reason enough to be baptized.

> When they heard this, they were **baptized** in the name of the **Lord Jesus**.
> - Acts 19:5

## Some believe they cannot live faithfully after baptism

If properly taught, one realizes he needs to be faithful to the Lord after baptism. Many voice their concern about living faithfully after having been baptized. Fearful of failure, they refuse.

It is at this point one needs to realize what God is calling for in His children, whether they are a new convert or a seasoned Christian.

1. **He calls for faithfulness.** John wrote, "Be _____ until death, and I will give you the crown of life" (Revelation 2:10). God expects His children to grow and mature (2 Peter 3:18), to sin less over time. Yet, He has never expected or called for sinless perfection. When a child of God sins (and they do), he is to _____ the sin, and God will be "_____ and _____ to forgive us" (1 John 1:9).

2. **He calls for humbleness.** Those who are humble Christians realize they have sinned, and therefore need to call upon God to forgive them. The Bible calls upon us to be "_____ with humility" (1 Peter 5:5). It also reminds us "God resists the _____, But gives grace to the _____" (James 4:6).

Do not let the fear of failure keep you from being baptized!

## Some believe they are condemning the dead

Here is how this works. As one is being taught God's plan of salvation, they begin to think about members of their family, or a close friend who

> If we **confess** our **sins**, He is faithful and righteous to **forgive** us our sins and to **cleanse** us from all unrighteousness.
>
> - 1 John 1:9

recently passed away. They realize their loved one did not obey God. Though the student knows what to do to be saved, and wants to, he does not. He feels as though he is betraying a loved one.

Such is not true. Having such feelings indicates one does not realize he is responsible for himself alone. The following verses demonstrate such to be accurate.

1. "But _____ who does wrong will be repaid for what _____ has done, and there is no partiality" (Colossians 3:25). Who is the "he" in this verse? _____
_____

2. "For we must all appear before the judgment seat of Christ, that each _____ may receive the things done in the body, according to what _____ has done, whether good or bad" (2 Corinthians 5:10). Who is the "one" and the "he" in this passage? _____
_____

3. "So then _____ of us shall give account of _____ to God" (Romans 14:12). How many people does the word "himself" include?

Read Luke 16:19-31 and respond to the following questions.

1. Both Lazarus and the rich man die. Lazarus is taken to "_____ bosom" (v. 22), while the rich man finds himself in a place of "_____" (v. 28).

2. What two requests did the rich man make, both of which were denied (v. 24)? _____
_____
_____

> So then **each one** of us will give an **account** of **himself** to God.
> - Romans 14:12

**LESSON 10** Why Do Some Wait?

3. How many living brothers did the rich man have (v. 28)? _____

4. What did the rich man not want for his brothers (v. 28)? _____
_____

If it be so that one has relatives or friends which were not obedient to God and have since passed away, the same statements of the rich man would be shared with you and me. An individual can be, and is, only responsible for himself.

## Some believe they do not know enough

Frequently, one puts off baptism because he does not feel he knows enough. Perhaps, he thinks he should have much more knowledge about the Bible than he presently does. Maybe he feels he should have more verses memorized.

Having Bible knowledge is great, and so is memorizing Scripture. But what does one really need to know before he is baptized? This is a great Bible question deserving of a great Bible answer.

Consider Acts 8:12 as the source to answer this question. "But when they believed Philip as he _____ the things concerning the _____ of God and the _____ of Jesus Christ, both men and women were _____." Philip preached about three matters.

1. **He preached about the kingdom of God.** In this text, the kingdom is a reference to the Lord's church (Matthew 16:18-19). The candidate for baptism must have a basic understanding of the Lord's church. It is to be understood there is only _____ body

> I also say to you that you are Peter, and upon this **rock** I will build **My church**; and the gates of **Hades** will not **overpower** it.
>
> - Matthew 16:18

> For by **one Spirit** we were all **baptized** into **one body**...
> - 1 Corinthians 12:13

(Ephesians 4:4), which is identified as the "church" (Ephesians 1:22-23). It is to be known the Lord will place the saved in the _____ (Acts 2:47). It is to be realized there is a connection between being _____ and being in the _____ (1 Corinthians 12:13).

2. **He preached about the authority of Jesus.** He made it known to the Samaritans Jesus had "_____ authority" (Matthew 28:18). Simply put, Philip was not commanding baptism because *he* thought they should do it, but because it was what *the Lord* commanded. Still today, we do what we do because Jesus is our authority.

3. **He preached about baptism.** The reader is forced to conclude Philip taught about the necessity of baptism since men and women came to be baptized.

One is a candidate for baptism as he realizes Jesus, who has all authority, has commanded baptism, and that the baptism will cause the Lord to add him to the one true church.

## Some believe they have enough time to do it later

Sadly, many put off baptism thinking they will have time and opportunity to do it at a later date. Some find the time; most do not. It is essential one understand life is brief, and unpredictable. The wise man wrote, "Do not boast about _____, For you do not _____ what a day may bring forth" (Proverbs 27:1). The Bible is full of reminders concerning the brevity of life. Match the verses on the left with the correct descriptions on the right.

**LESSON 10** Why Do Some Wait? 83

1. Job 7:6 \_\_\_\_\_ A vapor

2. 1 Samuel 20:3 \_\_\_\_\_ A swift ship

3. 2 Samuel 14:4 \_\_\_\_\_ A declining shadow

4. Job 7:7 \_\_\_\_\_ A step

5. James 4:14 \_\_\_\_\_ Grass and flowers

6. Psalm 102:11 \_\_\_\_\_ Spilled water

7. Job 9:26 \_\_\_\_\_ A weaver's shuttle

8. Psalm 103:15-16 \_\_\_\_\_ The wind

May the one in need of obedience to God's word see the need for immediate and swift action! Time has a way of running out.

## What will you do?

The question comes to you now. Will you reject these as reasons for not being baptized? Although some of these may start out looking like good reasons, none of them, in fact, are. Time is fleeting, and such is why Paul wrote, "Behold, _____ is the accepted time; behold, _____ is the day of salvation" (2 Corinthians 6:2). Will you now obey God?

## Some questions from our study

1. What did Saul accomplish by being baptized? _____
   _____

2. What two things does God call for after baptism? _____
   _____
   _____

3. What three things did Philip preach about? _____
   _____
   _____

4. List three ways the Bible describes the brevity of life. _____
   _____
   _____

# Now That You're a Christian

**Lesson 11**

Congratulations! You are now a member of the greatest family of all, the family of God! Your decision to become a Christian is a great one, but one that is accompanied by responsibility. In a sense, being baptized is just the beginning of a new, fantastic life. Now, God desires that you grow as a child of His. Growth does not occur all at once, but little by little, day by day.

## The Bible calls for growth

The word of God demands a new convert to grow. Standing still, or in one spot, is not an option. Consider the following.

1. Peter wrote, "as _____ babes, desire the pure _____ of the word, that you may _____ thereby" (1 Peter 2:2). The newborn in this verse is the new child of God. His desire should be to grow. Such is done by feasting on the milk of the word.

   A new child of God starts by learning the basic topics. He does not need to attempt trying to discover difficult topics or passages. Such might be too discouraging, perhaps drive a new convert away from God.

   Recall when Jesus offered the Great Commission, He said, "Go therefore and make disciples of all the nations, _____ them in the name of the Father and of the Son and of the Holy Spirit, _____ them to

> **Memory Verse**
>
> But **grow** in the **grace** and **knowledge** of our Lord and Savior **Jesus Christ**. To Him be the **glory** both **now** and **forever**. Amen.
>
> - 2 Peter 3:18

observe all things that I have commanded you; and lo, I am with you always, even to the end of the age. Amen" (Matthew 28:19-20).

There is teaching which is required after one has been baptized, and converted. This teaching begins with fundamental subjects of the Bible.

2. Again, the apostle penned, "but _____ in the grace and knowledge of our Lord and Savior Jesus Christ. To Him be the glory both now and forever. Amen" (2 Peter 3:18). Simply put, a new Christian must always be growing and developing as a person of God.

### How growth occurs

Development and improvement occur only when one is attached to a source providing the necessary ingredients for growth. Read John 15:1-8 and answer the following questions.

1. How did Jesus identify Himself? _____

2. What happens to the branch which does not bear fruit? _____

3. The branch, by itself, cannot do what unless attached to the vine? _____

4. What can one do without Jesus? _____

5. God is glorified as man does what? _____

The branches in this passage are individuals. This is seen in the use of the words "he," "him," and

> I am the **vine**, you are the **branches**; he who **abides** in Me and I in him, he bears much **fruit**, for apart from Me you can do **nothing**.
> 
> - John 15:5

"anyone." In order for the branch to survive, thrive and grow, it *must* be attached to the vine. Why? Because the vine offers the following benefits and advantages.

1.  **Nutrients.** Through the vine flows life-giving and life-sustaining nutrients. Jesus offers the same to those wishing to grow. "Blessed are those who _____ and thirst for righteousness, For they shall be _____" (Matthew 5:6).

2.  **Strength.** The vine lends strength to the branches. Growing is not always easy, and often there are pains associated with it. Jesus presents the same to those desiring to mature. "Come to Me, all you who _____ and are heavy laden, and I will give you _____" (Matthew 11:28).

3.  **Support.** The vine gives support when strong breezes blow in. Jesus provides the very same to those thirsty for growth. Paul identifies Jesus as the "_____" in 1 Corinthians 10:4. He is the Christian's solid foundation.

Without the proper nutrients, strength or support which Jesus and His word offer, one cannot grow. One who attaches himself to Jesus, the Vine, will grow exceptionally well.

## Adding to your faith

The Bible presents the ultimate blueprint for growth. It illuminates the pathway one travels to become the complete person of God.

This plan for growth is found in 2 Peter 1:5-7. It makes mention of seven things one adds to his faith. List them on the next page.

> ...all drank the same **spiritual drink**, for they were drinking from a spiritual **rock** which followed them; and the rock was **Christ**.
>
> - 1 Corinthians 10:4

1. _____
2. _____
3. _____
4. _____
5. _____
6. _____
7. _____

**Virtue** is moral excellence. It is the attitude of always wanting to do what is right, especially when no one is watching. The wise man wrote, "The _____ of the _____ will guide them, But the perversity of the unfaithful will destroy them" (Proverbs 11:3). New children of God strive to be moral, ethical people.

**Knowledge** is vital to the growing child of God. It comes only through hard and persistent work. Paul wrote, "Be _____ to present yourself approved to God, a worker who does not need to be ashamed, rightly dividing the _____ of truth" (2 Timothy 2:15). God's word must be opened daily (Acts 17:11). Hosea offers caution to those not willing to gain knowledge when he wrote God's people were "_____ for lack of _____" (Hosea 4:6).

> My people are **destroyed** for lack of **knowledge**...
> - Hosea 4:6

**Self-control** is the ability to show superior domination over things which are wrong. It is not always easy, nor is it always the most enjoyable. Consider Moses, who chose "to _____ affliction with the people of God than to enjoy the passing _____ of sin" (Hebrews 11:25). The person of God who is striving to grow must exhibit self-control.

**Perseverance** is the ability to last through difficult times. Challenging occasions will most certainly come for the new convert, and they will arrive in many different forms. Jesus said, "By your _____ possess your _____" (Luke 21:19). This patience is endurance.

**Godliness** indicates one has deep-rooted reverence and fear for God. So much so the new Christian will begin to do as God asks as a simple matter of respect. The wise man summed it up well when saying, "Let us hear the conclusion of the whole matter: _____ God, and _____ his commandments: for this is the whole duty of man" (Ecclesiastes 12:13).

**Brotherly love** is that special bond which only exists in the family of God. People of God who are growing spiritually will increase their love for their brethren. The following attitudes must be adopted. "And be ye _____ one to another, tenderhearted, _____ one another, even as God for Christ's sake hath forgiven you" (Ephesians 4:32). As a new child of God, this love will be one of the most special blessings.

**Love** is merely having the best interest of others in mind. This is especially true of your desire for others to go to Heaven. Others are not always easy to love, particularly when they have mistreated you. Nevertheless, it is a debt which each man owes his fellow man. "_____ no one anything except to _____ one another, for he who loves another has fulfilled the law" (Romans 13:8).

Notice the first five of these are goals involving you as an individual. They are attitudes which you will exclusively control. Brotherly love involves a relationship with a small circle of folks, while love

> Owe **nothing** to anyone except to **love** one another; for he who loves his **neighbor** has **fulfilled** the law.
>
> - Romans 13:8

encompasses your association with everyone. This illustrates God's desire for you to grow surely, steadily and outwardly.

## God wants you to be complete

God wants the very best for you. He desires that you grow and grow, day by day, becoming the most complete Christian you can be. Completion can only come if one is willing to grow.

1. As Paul concluded his last letter to church at Corinth, he offered several admonitions, among which was "become _____" (2 Corinthians 13:11).

2. Becoming complete cannot occur without help from God. Paul reminded us of this fact when writing, "being confident of this very thing, that He who has _____ a good work in you will _____ it until the day of Jesus Christ" (Philippians 1:6).

3. The Colossian letter encourages its readers, "stand _____ and _____ in all the will of God" (Colossians 4:12).

4. Completion comes as a result of devout investigation of God's word. The apostle taught, "All Scripture is given by _____ of God, and is _____ for doctrine, for reproof, for correction, for instruction in righteousness, that the man of God may be _____, thoroughly equipped for every good work" (2 Timothy 3:16-17).

5. James calls our attention to the fact completion comes not overnight, but through hard work

> And let **endurance** have its **perfect** result, so that you may be perfect and **complete**, lacking in nothing.
> - James 1:4

**LESSON 11** Now That You're a Christian

over time. He wrote "But let _____ have its perfect work, that you may be _____ and _____, lacking nothing" (James 1:4).

## So let's grow

Great and wonderful blessings are yours to enjoy as a Christian! Even better and more eternal rewards await those who are willing to work long and hard to grow. Adopt the following attitude. "I press toward the goal for the prize of the upward call of God in Christ Jesus" (Philippians 3:14).

## Some questions from our study

1. What does it mean to desire the milk of the word? _____
   _____
   _____

2. What three important services does the vine provide to the branches?
   _____
   _____
   _____

3. What seven things is one to add to his faith? _____
   _____
   _____
   _____
   _____

## Lesson 12

# Responsibilities of a Christian

It is a wonderful privilege to be a Christian! It is a life filled with blessings and benefits given by the Lord (Ephesians 1:3, James 1:17). Along with these gifts comes a measure of responsibility. These obligations belong to each individual Christian. Each disciple must make himself aware of what they are, and then be diligent in keeping them. This lesson outlines those tasks.

## A Christian's responsibility to God

A faithful child of God is one who understands his responsibilities, and remains consistent in the discharge of them. He realizes these are obligations to God which must be kept. Think about the following areas in which a Christian should be faithful.

1. **Be faithful in attendance.** Hebrews 10:25 reports, "not _____ the _____ of ourselves together, as is the manner of some, but exhorting one another, and so much the more as you see the Day approaching." A Christian is part of a wonderful family, and should desire to be with them at every opportunity. It is a good thing to assemble with the saints regularly. We are taught, "Therefore, to him who knows to do _____ and does not do it, to him it is _____" (James 4:17). A failure to congregate with God's people is an indication of deeper rooted problems.

> **Memory Verse**
>
> Therefore, my beloved brethren, be **steadfast**, **immovable**, always **abounding** in the **work** of the Lord, knowing that your **labor** is not in **vain** in the **Lord**.
>
> - 1 Corinthians 15:58

> ...when you **read** you can **understand** my insight into the **mystery** of **Christ**.
>
> - Ephesians 3:4

2. **Be faithful in worship.** God calls upon His people to worship Him in _____ and in _____ (John 4:24). It is the responsibility of a Christian to partake of the Lord's supper each first day of the week (Acts 20:7) and also to give (1 Corinthians 16:1-2). Consistently observing the Lord's Supper and contributing to the Lord makes one obedient and responsible in his duties to God.

3. **Be faithful in the study of God's word.** A child of God's day is not complete without the study of the Bible, because he knows in reading he may _____ (Ephesians 3:4). He studies regularly so that he can determine what is truth and what is not (Acts 17:11, 2 Timothy 2:15). Studying results in the acquisition of knowledge to discern and not accept false teaching.

4. **Be faithful to God and His word.** A child of God is called upon to be "_____ until death, and I will give you the crown of _____" (Revelation 2:10). Even though Christians strive to do their very best, they sin from time to time.

   If it is a private matter between God and self, they should confess the wrong to God. John wrote, "If we confess our _____, He is faithful and just to _____ us our sins and to _____ us from all unrighteousness" (1 John 1:9).

   If it involves sin which is publicly known, then one should feel moved to "_____ your trespasses to one another, and _____ for one another, that you may be healed. The effective, fervent prayer of a righteous man avails _____" (James 5:16).

5. **Be faithful to the Lord's work.** There is an abundance of work needing to be done in the Lord's church. When it comes time to help labor for the Lord, a Christian always stands up to say he is ready. Recall when Jesus said, "The harvest truly is plentiful, but the laborers are _____" (Matthew 9:37).

A good motto for the Christian is, "I am ready!" We must take up the same attitude presented in 1 Corinthians 15:58. "Therefore, my beloved brethren, be _____, immovable, always abounding in the _____ of the Lord, knowing that your labor is not in _____ in the Lord."

## A Christian's responsibility to God's family

Christians share an amazing relationship with the family of God. There is a special love and bond which exists in the family of God which occurs nowhere else. Each individual child of God is responsible for acting thoughtfully of his fellow children of God. A study of the phrase "one another" will serve to show what these responsibilities are. Locate the following verses and write down what Christians should do or be for one another.

1. John 13:34 _____
2. Romans 12:10 _____
3. Romans 12:16 _____
4. Romans 15:5 _____
5. Romans 15:7 _____
6. Romans 15:14 _____

> Be **devoted** to one another in **brotherly love**; give **preference** to one another in **honor**.
>
> - Romans 12:10

> Be **kind** to one another, **tender-hearted**, **forgiving** each other, just as God in Christ also has **forgiven** you.
>
> - Ephesians 4:32

7. Romans 16:16 _____
8. Galatians 5:13 _____
9. Ephesians 4:2 _____
10. Ephesians 4:32 _____
11. Ephesians 5:19 _____
12. Ephesians 5:21 _____
13. 1 Thessalonians 4:18 _____
14. 1 Thessalonians 5:11 _____
15. Hebrews 3:13 _____
16. Hebrews 10:24 _____
17. 1 Peter 4:9 _____
18. 1 Peter 4:10 _____

It is easy to see Christians have a tremendous responsibility in caring for and loving each other. It is not to be taken lightly or casually.

### A Christian's responsibility to himself

While it is good for a child of God to understand his responsibility to other Christians, he must also be aware of obligations he has to himself. Consider these four commands.

1. **Take heed to yourself.** Paul wrote, "Take _____ to yourself and to the doctrine. Continue in them, for in doing this you will save both _____ and those who hear you" (1 Timothy 4:16). A Christian is responsible for himself first. If he cannot save himself, he will be of no help to others.

2. **Keep yourself pure.** Timothy was charged, "keep yourself _____" (1 Timothy 5:22). A

Christian needs to behave himself, keeping his mind (or heart) clean. This means he needs to be very selective in what he reads, what he watches, what he listens to and with whom he keeps company (1 Corinthians 15:33).

3. **Consider yourself.** The Galatian brethren were told to help restore those who have fallen away from the Lord, but to also be "_____ yourself lest you also be _____" (Galatians 6:1). This warning is issued to those who would be tempted to think too highly of themselves (Romans 12:3), or those who think they are no longer capable of committing sin (1 Corinthians 10:12).

4. **Examine yourself.** The only way to determine one's spiritual status is to conduct an examination. Paul said, "_____ yourselves as to whether you are in the faith" (2 Corinthians 13:5). This is a head-to-toe examination which should be carried out daily to ensure one's standing with God.

## A Christian's responsibility regarding the world

A Christian has no choice but to physically dwell in this world. The world can be a very dangerous place for God's children if not handled carefully. The Bible is very careful to warn God's people about the world. Search the following passages and make a note of what it teaches regarding the Christian and his relationship with the world.

1. Matthew 5:14; Philippians 2:15 _____
   _____

2. Romans 12:2 _____
   _____

> You are the **light** of the **world**. A **city** set on a **hill** cannot be **hidden**.
> - Matthew 5:14

> Do not **love** the **world** nor the things in the world. If anyone loves the world, the **love** of the **Father** is **not** in him.
>
> - 1 John 2:15

3. James 1:27 _____
   _____

4. James 4:4 _____
   _____

5. 1 John 2:15 _____
   _____

In addition to these thoughts, people of God must also be very cautious with whom they keep company. Think seriously about the following passages.

Paul warned his Corinthian brethren, "Do not be deceived: Evil _____ corrupts good _____" (1 Corinthians 15:33). It is very easy to be tricked into thinking bad company will not affect an individual.

Solomon made it very simple to understand when he wrote, "He who walks with wise men will be _____, But the companion of fools will be _____" (Proverbs 13:20).

As an example, ponder the life of Demas, who once was championed by the apostle Paul as a "fellow laborer" (Philemon 24). Yet later, Paul made the sad announcement that "Demas has _____ me, having loved this present world, and has _____" (2 Timothy 4:10).

While the Christian has a duty to spread the gospel, and to be a good influence upon the world, he also must refuse to let the world penetrate his spiritual well-being.

## Taking the responsibility seriously

May each one blessed to be called a Christian undertake his responsibilities seriously. The eternal

## LESSON 12 Responsibilities of a Christian

rewards for doing such far outweigh any temporary setbacks one might experience in this world.

## Some questions from our study

1. What responsibilities does a Christians have to God? _____
   _____
   _____
   _____

2. List at least five duties each child of God has to his spiritual family.
   _____
   _____
   _____
   _____
   _____

3. What obligations does a Christian have to himself? _____
   _____
   _____

4. Why must a child of God be careful how he interacts with the world?
   _____
   _____
   _____

**Lesson 13**

# Helping Others Become Christians

As this study draws to a conclusion, it is important to make note of one other solemn duty of a child of God. Such is the joy and bliss of helping others become Christians. Though increase comes as a result of God, the seed must be planted and watered by His people (1 Corinthians 3:6). This lesson is designed to illustrate the ways you can be of spiritual help to others.

## Finding others in need of salvation

Helping others begins with finding others. It could be a member of your family, or a friend with whom you are familiar. It may be your co-worker, or even a stranger you encounter in passing. Most everybody you meet is in need of God and of salvation from sin.

Read John 1:40-42 and answer the following questions.

1. What was the name of Simon Peter's brother who had heard John speak and had followed him? _____
2. Who did he find first? _____
3. What did he announce to the one he found? _____ _____
4. In the early part of v. 42, who did he bring him to? _____

It is up to obedient believers to begin finding others who can be led to Jesus the Christ. Sadly, not

> **Memory Verse**
>
> And the things that you have **heard** from me among many **witnesses**, commit these to **faithful** men who will be able to **teach** others also.
>
> - 2 Timothy 2:2

> He found first his own **brother** Simon and said to him, "We have **found** the **Messiah**" (which translated means Christ). He **brought** him to **Jesus**.
>
> - John 1:41-42

everyone will be interested, but always remember persistence pays off.

In the blanks provided below, write down five names of those who are not Christians. Once finished, begin making plans to "find them" and "bring them to Jesus."

1. _____
2. _____
3. _____
4. _____
5. _____

## Understanding the teaching chain

For centuries, men have been directing other men to Jesus. It is a chain of teaching which is intended to never stop. You have become part of that chain. It has become part of your responsibility to guide another in becoming a child of God.

The apostle penned, "And the things that you have _____ from me among many witnesses, _____ these to faithful men who will be able to _____ others also" (2 Timothy 2:2).

Over the years, some men have failed in sustaining this chain. As a consequence, a generation of a family grew up not knowing about God. Let the chain of teaching continue with you.

## Becoming a soul winner

The wise man wrote, "The fruit of the righteous is a tree of life, And he who _____ souls is _____" (Proverbs 11:30).

## LESSON 13 Helping Others Become Christians

Becoming a successful soul-winner requires several acknowledgements on your part. Consider.

1. **All men have a soul.** Jesus once said, "And do not fear those who kill the _____ but cannot kill the _____. But rather fear Him who is able to destroy both soul and body in hell" (Matthew 10:28). It is to be understood that our physical bodies are temporary, and are able to be destroyed. However, our soul, while invisible, is eternal in nature (2 Corinthians 4:18).

2. **All men have a soul which is valuable.** Again the Lord asked, "For what _____ is it to a man if he gains the whole _____, and loses his own _____? Or what will a man give in _____ for his soul?" (Matthew 16:26). The most valuable possession each man has is his soul. The answer to Jesus' question is: the man has gained nothing and lost everything.

3. **All men have a soul proceeding to Heaven or Hell.** As Jesus described the judgment, He said, "And these will go away into everlasting _____, but the righteous into eternal _____" (Matthew 25:46). A soul is of great value and to be treasured.

> ...for the things which are **seen** are **temporal**, but the things which are **not seen** are **eternal**.
>
> - 2 Corinthians 4:18

Since these things are true, those who have begun a relationship with God through baptism should feel compelled to become a soul winner. Will you?

## Leading others to Jesus through influence

One of the very best ways you can help others become a Christian is through influence, or example. While others might ignore what you say, it is very difficult to disregard what you do. Never forget this!

> ...**rejoicing** in hope, **persevering** in tribulation, **devoted** to prayer...
>
> - Romans 12:12

The following attitudes just might be what causes one to reconsider their need for God in their life.

1. **Patience in tribulation.** Christians are commanded to be such in Romans 12:12. Tribulation comes in many different and various forms. In its most basic sense, tribulation is "a pressure or burden" placed upon an individual. Make a list below of events in this life which could bring about these pressures or burdens.

   _____
   _____
   _____
   _____

2. **Strength during persecution.** Upon the mount the Lord said, "Blessed are those who are _____ for righteousness' sake, For theirs is the kingdom of heaven. Blessed are you when they _____ and persecute you, and say all kinds of evil against you falsely for My sake. _____ and be exceedingly glad, for great is your reward in heaven, for so they persecuted the prophets who were before you" (Matthew 5:10-12). Without doubt, remaining strong and steadfast under persecution will have an impact on others.

3. **Consistency of holiness.** Those who wish to bring trouble upon Christians gain the victory when the believers stop living holily. Being constant and steady in attendance, Bible study and worship will attract the attention of others in time.

   Peter, to the wives of unbelievers, said the unbelieving husbands may be "won by the _____ of their wives, when they observe your _____ conduct accompanied by _____" (1 Peter 3:1-2). What is said here of wives is true of us all. The Christian's consistent life of holiness can, and will, draw unbelievers to God.

## Will you mention Christ to others?

Many years ago, James Rowe, wrote the following lyrics to the song entitled, "You Never Mentioned Him to Me." They are worthy of consideration.

> "When in the better land before the bar we stand,
> How deeply grieved our souls will be;
> If any lost one there should cry in deep despair,
> 'You never mentioned Him to me.'"

> "O let us spread the word where e'er it may be heard,
> Help groping souls the light to see,
> That yonder none may say, 'You showed me not the way.'
> You never mentioned Him to me."

> "A few sweet words may guide a lost one to His side,
> Or turn sad eyes on Calvary;
> So work as days go by, that yonder none may cry,
> 'You never mentioned Him to me.'"

> "You never mentioned Him to me,
> You helped me not the way to see;
> You met me day by day and knew I was astray,
> Yet never mentioned Him to me."

As children of God, it is our sincere obligation to introduce others to the Lord and Savior. May it never be said of you, or of any Christian: "You never mentioned Him to me!"

## Some questions from our study

1. Who did Andrew find and bring to Jesus? _____

2. What does a wise man do according to Proverbs 11:30? _____

3. What were the three facts we studied concerning the soul of man?

4. List the three ways a Christian can be a good influence on an unbeliever. _____

www.ingramcontent.com/pod-product-compliance
Lightning Source LLC
Chambersburg PA
CBHW070450050426
42451CB00015B/3419